W9-AAJ-885

ACADEMIC SKILLS PROBLEMS WORKBOOK

Academic Skills Problems Workbook

Edward S. Shapiro, PhD

THE GUILFORD PRESS
New York London

© 1996 The Guilford Press
A Division of Guilford Publications, Inc.
72 Spring Street, New York, NY 10012

All rights reserved

No part of this book may be reproduced, stored in a retrieval system, or transmitted, in any form or by any means, electronic, mechanical, photocopying, microfilming, recording, or otherwise, without written permission from the Publisher.

Printed in the United States of America

This book is printed on acid-free paper.

Last digit is print number: 9 8 7 6 5 4 3

ISBN 1-57230-107-4

LIMITED PHOTOCOPY LICENSE

The publisher grants to individual purchasers of this book nonassignable permission to reproduce handouts and forms in this book for personal use in clinical practice and not for resale or distribution.

These materials are intended for use only by qualified professionals. This license is limited to you and does not extend to other individuals. The license does not grant the right to reproduce these materials for other purposes (including but not limited to books, pamphlets, articles, video or audio tapes, and handouts or slides for lectures or workshops). Permission to reproduce these materials for these and any other purposes must be obtained in writing from Guilford Publications.

Contents

STEP 2. ASSESSING CURRICULUM PLACEMENT

STEP 3. INSTRUCTIONAL MODIFICATION

STEP 4. PROGRESS MONITORING

Introduction

The purpose of this workbook is to provide forms, instructions, and other materials to supplement *Academic Skills Problems: Direct Assessment and Intervention* (2nd edition). The workbook offers elaboration and detail of some of the material covered in the text, and also provides additional forms to supplement those in the text. Some forms in the text are duplicated in the workbook for ease in copying; users of the manual are granted permission from the publisher to copy and modify these forms for their personal use. Although the workbook can certainly be used on its own, its purpose is to complement rather than stand independent from the text.

The workbook also offers opportunities for learning, practicing, and mastering many of the skills discussed in the text. For example, a complete manual related to use of the Behavioral Observation of Students in Schools (B.O.S.S.) observation code is provided. Full definitions of the B.O.S.S. behavioral categories, as well as instructions for collecting information, scoring the observations, and interpreting the data, are given. Also included are forms for completing teacher and student interviews, along with a useful checklist for obtaining teacher reports of academic behavior.

In the area of conducting the direct assessment of academic skills, the workbook offers additional instructions and practice exercises in how these procedures are used. In particular, detailed explanations of using such measures as "digits correct per minute" and "correct letter sequences" to score math and spelling, respectively, are provided. The workbook also offers a description of and exercises in how to graph data, collect local norms, and other tasks related to direct assessment of academic skills.

The workbook follows the model of assessment described in the *Academic Skills Problems* text and depicted in Figure 1. The first section, corresponding to the first step of the assessment process—assessing the academic environment (see Figure 2)—provides materials for

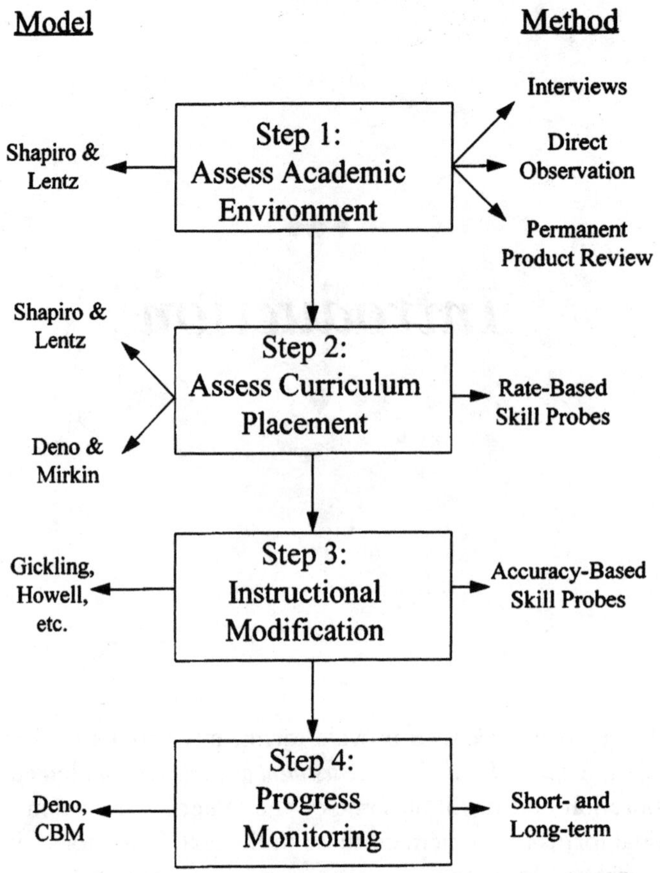

FIGURE 1. Model of direct assessment of academic skills.

interviewing teachers and students, conducting direct observations, and using informant report data (teacher rating scale). The next section, corresponding to Step 2 of the process—assessing curriculum placement—provides information related to the processes involved in direct assessment of academic skills (in particular, details about the assessment of reading, math, spelling, and written language). This section contains information on both the use of short- and long-term data collection procedures.

The third section of the workbook offers details on the use of a powerful instructional intervention, the "folding-in" technique. The final section, corresponding to Step 4 of the model—progress monitoring—provides important information about the graphic display of data, as well as the collection of local norms.

Throughout, the reader will find detailed "how to" explanations offered in a step-by-step fashion. Practice exercises are also provided, and readers are encouraged to develop their own exercises modeled on those in the workbook.

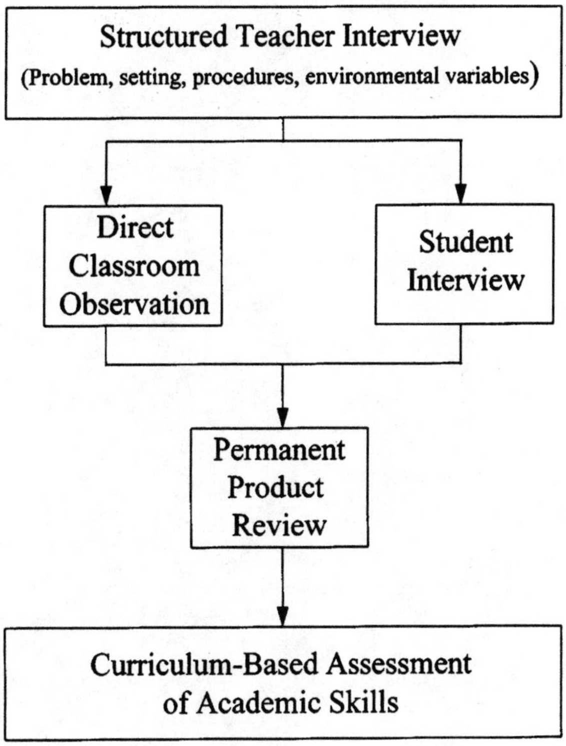

FIGURE 2. Sequence of methods in conducting Steps 1 and 2 of the direct assessment of academic skills.

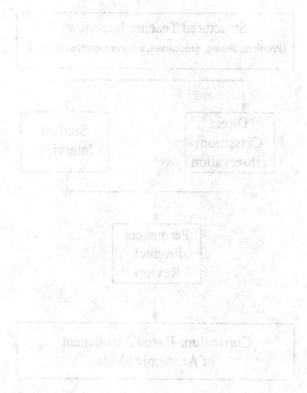

STEP 1

♦♦♦

Assessing the Academic Environment

♦

♦♦♦

Teacher Interview

♦

The assessment process begins with the teacher interview. Several forms are provided to facilitate the interview. The first, which is also printed in the text, suggests the specific questions that should be addressed for each academic area. Designed primarily to be completed during a face-to-face meeting with a teacher, the form can also be given to the teacher to fill out before the interview actually occurs. When the form is used in this way, the information provided by the teacher can be used as the context for more in-depth discussion.

TEACHER INTERVIEW FORM FOR ACADEMIC PROBLEMS

Student: ______________________ **Teacher:** ______________________

Birthdate: ______________________ **Date:** ______________________

Grade: _____ **School:** ______________________

Interviewer: ______________________

GENERAL

Why was this student referred? ______________________________________

____

What type(s) of academic problem(s) does this student have?

____

READING

Primary type of reading series used
- ☐ Basal reader
- ☐ Literature-based
- ☐ Trade books

Secondary type of reading materials used
- ☐ Basal reader
- ☐ Literature-based
- ☐ Trade books
- ☐ None

Reading series title (if applicable) ______________________________

Grade level of series currently placed ______________________________

Title of book in series currently placed ______________________________

How many groups do you teach? ______________________________

Which group is this student assigned to? ______________________________

At this point in the school year, where is the average student in your class reading?

Level and book ______________________________

Place in book (begginning, middle, end, specific page) ______________________________

Time allotted/day for reading ______________________________

How is time divided? (Independent seatwork? Small group? Cooperative groups?)

____

____

How is placement in reading program determined? ________________________________

____

How are changes made in the program? ________________________________

____

Does this student participate in Chapter I (remedial) reading programs? How much?

____

Typical daily instructional procedures ________________________________

____

Contingencies for accuracy? ________________________________

____

Contingencies for completion? ________________________________

____

Daily scores (if available) for past two weeks ________________________________

____

Group standardized test results (if available) ________________________________

____

ORAL READING

How does he/she read orally, compared to others in his/her reading group?

___ Much worse ___ Somewhat worse ___ About the same

___ Somewhat better ___ Much better

In the class?

___ Much worse ___ Somewhat worse ___ About the same

___ Somewhat better ___ Much better

WORD ATTACK

Does he/she attempt unknown words? ________________________________

SIGHT WORDS

How is the student's sight vocabulary, compared to others in his/her reading group?

___ Much worse ___ Somewhat worse ___ About the same

___ Somewhat better ___ Much better

In the class?

___ Much worse ___ Somewhat worse ___ About the same

___ Somewhat better ___ Much better

COMPREHENSION

How well does the student seem to understand what he/she reads, compared to others in his/her reading group?

___ Much worse ___ Somewhat worse ___ About the same

___ Somewhat better ___ Much better

In the class?

___ Much worse ___ Somewhat worse ___ About the same

___ Somewhat better ___ Much better

BEHAVIOR DURING READING

Rate the following areas from 1 to 5 (1 = very unsatisfactory, 3 = satisfactory, 5 = superior)

Reading Group

a. Oral reading ability (as evidenced in reading group) ____
b. Volunteers answers ____
c. When called upon, gives correct answer ____
d. Attends to other students when they read aloud ____
e. Knows the appropriate place in book ____

Independent Seatwork

a. Stays on task ____
b. Completes assigned work in required time ____
c. Work is accurate ____
d. Works quietly ____
e. Remains in seat when required ____

HOMEWORK (if any)

a. Handed in on time ____
b. Is complete ____
c. Is accurate ____

MATHEMATICS

Curriculum series ______________________________

What are the specific problems in math? ______________________________

____

Time allotted/day for math ______________________________

How is time divided? (Independent seatwork? Small group? Large group? Cooperative groups?) ______________________________

____

For an average-performing student in your class, at what point in the planned course format would you consider this student at mastery?
(See computational mastery form, p. 15.) ______________________________

For an average-performing student in your class, at what point in the planned course format would you consider this student instructional?
(See computational mastery form.) ______________________________

For an average-performing student in your class, at what point in the planned course format would you consider this student frustrational?
(See computational mastery form.) ______________________________

For the targeted student in your class, at what point in the planned course format would you consider this student at mastery?
(See computational mastery form.) ______________________________

For the targeted student in your class, at what point in the planned course format would you consider this student instructional?
(See computational mastery form.) ______________________________

For the targeted student in your class, at what point in the planned course format would you consider this student frustrational?
(See computational mastery form.) ______________________________

How is mastery assessed? ______________________________

Describe any difficulties this student has in applying math skills (measurement, time, money, geometry, problem solving) ______________________________

____

Are your students grouped in math? ______________________________

If so, how many groups do you have, and in which group is this student placed? ______________________________

____

How are changes made in the student's math program? ________________________

____

Does this student participate in Chapter I (remedial) math programs? ____________

Typical daily instructional procedures ______________________________

____

Contingencies for accuracy? ______________________________________

Contingencies for completion? ____________________________________

Daily scores (if available) for past 2 weeks __________________________

____

Group standardized test results (if available) _________________________

____

BEHAVIOR DURING MATH

Rate the following areas from 1 to 5 (1 = very unsatisfactory, 3 = satisfactory, 5 = superior)

Math Group (large)

a. Volunteers answers ____
b. When called upon, gives correct answer ____
c. Attends to other students when they give answers ____
d. Knows the appropriate place in math book ____

Math Group (small)

a. Volunteers answers ____
b. When called upon, gives correct answer ____
c. Attends to other students when they give answers ____
d. Knows the appropriate place in math book ____

Math Group (cooperative)

a. Volunteers answers ____
b. Contributes to group objectives ____
c. Attends to other students when they give answers ____
d. Facilitates others in group to participate ____
e. Shows appropriate social skills in group ____

Independent Seatwork

a. Stays on task ____
b. Completes assigned work in required time ____
c. Work is accurate ____
d. Works from initial directions ____
e. Works quietly ____
f. Remains in seat when required ____

Homework (if any)

a. Handed in on time ____
b. Is complete ____
c. Is accurate ____

SPELLING

Type of material used for spelling instruction:

☐ Published spelling series
Title of series ______________________________

☐ Basal reading series
Title of series ______________________________

☐ Teacher-made materials

☐ Other ______________________________

Level of instruction (if applicable) ______________________________

At this point in the school year, where is the average student in your class spelling?

Level, place in book ______________________________

Time allotted/day for spelling ______________________________

How is time divided? (Independent seatwork? Small group? Cooperative groups?)

____

____

How is placement in spelling program determined? ______________________________

____

How are changes made in the program? ______________________________

____

Typical daily instructional procedures ______________________________

____

Contingencies for accuracy? ____________________

____

Contingencies for completion? ____________________

____

WRITING

Please describe the type of writing assignments you give ____________________

____

Compared to others in your class, does he/she have difficulty with (please provide brief descriptions):

- ☐ Expressing thoughts ____________________
- ☐ Story length ____________________
- ☐ Story depth ____________________
- ☐ Creativity ____________________

Mechanics:

- ☐ Capitalization
- ☐ Punctuation
- ☐ Grammar
- ☐ Handwriting
- ☐ Spelling

BEHAVIOR

Are there social/behavioral adjustment problems interfering with this student's academic progress? (be specific)

____

____

Check any item that describes this student's behavior:

_____ Distracted, short attention span, unable to concentrate
_____ Hyperactive, constant, aimless movement
_____ Impulsive/aggressive behaviors, lacks self-control
_____ Fluctuating levels of performance
_____ Frequent negative self-statements
_____ Unconsciously repeating verbal or motor acts
_____ Lethargic, sluggish, too quiet
_____ Difficulty sharing or working with others

ELEMENTARY MATH WHOLE NUMBER COMPUTATIONAL SKILLS EXPECTED MASTERY

GRADE 1

1. Add two one-digit numbers: sums to 10
2. Subtract two one-digit numbers: combinations to 10

GRADE 2

3. Add two one-digit numbers: sums 11 to 19
4. Add a one-digit number to a two-digit number—no regrouping
5. Add a two-digit number to a two-digit number—no regrouping
6. Add a three digit number to a three-digit number—no regrouping
7. Subtract a one-digit number from a one or two digit number: combinations to 18
8. Subtract a one-digit number from a two-digit number—no regrouping
9. Subtract a two-digit number from a two-digit number—no regrouping
10. Subtract a three-digit number from a three-digit number—no regrouping
11. Multiplication facts—0's, 1's, 2's

GRADE 3

12. Add three or more one-digit numbers
13. Add three or more two-digit numbers—no regrouping
14. Add three or more three and four-digit numbers—no regrouping
15. Add a one-digit number to a two-digit number with regrouping
16. Add a two-digit number to a two-digit number with regrouping
17. Add a three-digit number to a three-digit number with regrouping
18. Add a two-digit number to a three-digit number with regrouping from the tens column only
19. Add a two-digit number to a three-digit number with regrouping from the hundreds column only
20. Add a three-digit number to a three-digit number with regrouping from the tens column only
21. Add a three-digit number to a three-digit number with regrouping from the hundreds column only
22. Add a three-digit number to a three-digit number with regrouping from the tens and hundreds columns
23. Add a four-digit number to a four-digit number with regrouping in one to three columns
24. Subtract two four-digit numbers—no regrouping
25. Subtract a one-digit number from a two-digit number with regrouping
26. Subtract a two-digit number from a two-digit number with regrouping
27. Subtract a two-digit number from a three-digit number with regrouping from tens column only

28. Subtract a two-digit number from a three-digit number with regrouping from hundreds column only
29. Subtract a two-digit number from a three-digit number with regrouping from tens and hundreds columns
30. Subtract a three-digit number from a three-digit number with regrouping from tens column only
31. Subtract a three-digit number from a three-digit number with regrouping from hundreds column only
32. Subtract a three-digit number from a three-digit number with regrouping from tens and hundreds columns
33. Multiplication facts—3 to 9

GRADE 4

34. Add a five or six-digit number to a five or six-digit number with regrouping in any columns
35. Add three or more two-digit numbers with regrouping
36. Add three or more three-digit numbers with regrouping
37. Subtract a five or six-digit number from a five or six-digit number with regrouping in any columns
38. Multiply a two-digit number by a one-digit number—no regrouping
39. Multiply a three-digit number by a one-digit number—no regrouping
40. Multiply a two-digit number by a one-digit number with regrouping
41. Multiply a three-digit number by a one-digit number with regrouping
42. Division facts—0 to 9
43. Divide a two-digit number by a one-digit number—no regrouping
44. Divide a two-digit number by a one-digit number with remainder
45. Divide a three-digit number by a one-digit number with remainder
46. Divide a four-digit number by a one-digit number with remainder

GRADE 5

47. Multiply a two-digit number by a two-digit number with regrouping
48. Multiply a three-digit number by a two-digit number with regrouping
49. Multiply a three-digit number by a three-digit number with regrouping

Interviews with teachers should be guided by the need to obtain general information about how a teacher manages instruction and the classroom environment. As such, a more general interview format can be used. This format should include questions about instructional practices, curriculum, assessment, and management. Typically, the interview is conducted after an observation of the teacher teaching the student of interest. The questions on page 18 are useful to guide this type of interview process.

QUESTIONS TO GUIDE GENERAL TEACHER INTERVIEWS FOR ACADEMIC SKILLS*

Teacher ______________________ **Student** ______________________
Subject(s) ______________________ **Date** ______________________

1. What was the specific instructional assignment being taught during my observation?
2. How was the instructional assignment presented to the students?
3. What opportunities were presented for guided practice?
4. What opportunities were presented for independent practice?
5. What opportunities were presented for feedback to students?
6. What were the specific objectives of the instructional lesson observed?
7. How did you determine whether students were successful during the lesson observed?
8. What type of additional support beyond your normal classroom instruction does this student need to succeed?
9. What strategies seem to work with this student?
10. What strategies do not seem to work with this student?
11. What types of assessment information do you collect?
12. How do you use the information gathered about student performance?
13. During group instruction, what clues do you use to evaluate a student's performance?
14. What adaptations do you make or permit of assignments?
15. What adaptations do you make or permit on tests?

*Many thanks to Christine Schubel, Ed.S., for her contributions to this form.

Academic Performance Rating Scale

Another approach to gathering information about student academic performance and classroom structure is to use a teacher rating scale. DuPaul, Rapport, and Perriello (1991) developed the Academic Performance Rating Scale (APRS), designed to provide teacher-based ratings of student performance in math and language arts among students in grades 1 through 6. The factor analysis of the scale results in three subscales: Academic Success, Impulse Control, and Academic Productivity (as judged by the teacher) (see Table 1). Normative data divided by gender, along with instructions for scoring for each factor, are provided (see Table 2).

ACADEMIC PERFORMANCE RATING SCALE*

Student ____________________ **Date** ________________

Age ____ **Grade** __________ **Teacher** ________________

For each of the items below, please estimate the above student's performance over the PAST WEEK. For each item, please circle one choice only.

1. Estimate the percentage of written **math work** completed (regardless of accuracy) relative to classmates.	0–49% 1	50–69% 2	70–79% 3	80–89% 4	90–100% 5
2. Estimate the percentage of written **language arts** work completed (regardless of accuracy) relative to classmates.	0–49% 1	50–69% 2	70–79% 3	80–89% 4	90–100% 5
3. Estimate the accuracy of completed written **math** work (i.e., percent correct of work done).	0–64% 1	65–69% 2	70–79% 3	80–89% 4	90–100% 5
4. Estimate the accuracy of completed written **language arts** work (i.e., percent correct of work done).	0–64% 1	65–69% 2	70–79% 3	80–89% 4	90–100% 5
5. How consistent has the quality of this child's academic work been over the past week?	Consistently poor 1	More poor than successful 2	Variable 3	More successful than poor 4	Consistently successful 5
6. How frequently does the student accurately follow teacher instructions and/or class discussion during *large-group* (e.g., whole class) instruction?	Never 1	Rarely 2	Sometimes 3	Often 4	Very often 5
7. How frequently does the student accurately follow teacher instructions and/or class discussion during *small-group* (e.g., reading group) instruction?	Never 1	Rarely 2	Sometimes 3	Often 4	Very often 5
8. How quickly does this child learn new material (i.e., pick up novel concepts)?	Very slowly 1	slowly 2	Average 3	Quickly 4	Very Quickly 5

(*continued*)

9. What is the quality or neatness of this child's handwriting?	Poor 1	Fair 2	Average 3	Above average 4	Excellent 5
10. What is the quality of this child's reading skills?	Poor 1	Fair 2	Average 3	Above average 4	Excellent 5
11. What is the quality of this child's writing skills?	Poor 1	Fair 2	Average 3	Above average 4	Excellent 5
12. How often does the child complete written work in a careless, hasty fashion?	Never 1	Rarely 2	Sometimes 3	Often 4	Very often 5
13. How frequently does the child take more time to complete work than his/her classmates?	Never 1	Rarely 2	Sometimes 3	Often 4	Very often 5
14. How often is the child able to pay attention without you prompting him/her?	Never 1	Rarely 2	Sometimes 3	Often 4	Very often 5
15. How frequently does this child require your assistance to accurately complete his/her academic work?	Never 1	Rarely 2	Sometimes 3	Often 4	Very often 5
16. How often does the child begin written work prior to understanding the directions?	Never 1	Rarely 2	Sometimes 3	Often 4	Very often 5
17. How frequently does this child have difficulty recalling material from a previous day's lessons?	Never 1	Rarely 2	Sometimes 3	Often 4	Very often 5
18. How often does the child appear to be staring excessively or "spaced out"?	Never 1	Rarely 2	Sometimes 3	Often 4	Very often 5
19. How often does the child appear withdrawn or tend to lack an emotional response in a social situation	Never 1	Rarely 2	Sometimes 3	Often 4	Very often 5

*From "Teacher Ratings of Academic Skills: The Development of the Academic Performance Rating Scale," by G. J. DuPaul, M. D. Rapport, and L. M. Perriello, 1991, *School Psychology Review, 20*, pp. 299–300. Copyright 1991 by National Association of School Psychologists. Reprinted by permission.

APRS Scoring Instructions:

Step 1: Write in the score assigned by the teacher for each item in the blank column.

Step 2: Sum the columns and write the total in the last row.

Item #	Academic Success	Impulse Control	Academic Productivity
1			
2			
3			
4			
5			
6			
7			
8			
9			
10			
11			
12			
13			
14			
15			
16			
17			
18			
19			
TOTALS	Academic Success score	Impulse Control score	Academic Productivity score

TABLE 1 Factor Structure of the Academic Performance Rating Scale (APRS)*

Scale item	Academic Success	Impulse Control	Academic Productivity
1. Math work completed	.30	−.02	**.84**
2. Language arts completed	.32	.06	**.82**
3. Math work accuracy	**.68**	.17	**.50**
4. Language arts accuracy	**.68**	.17	**.50**
5. Consistency of work	**.50**	.21	**.72**
6. Follows group instructions	.41	.35	**.69**
7. Follows small-group instructions	.39	.37	**.64**
8. Learns material quickly	**.81**	.17	.39
9. Neatness of handwriting	.41	**.50**	.31
10. Quality of reading	**.87**	.16	.23
11. Quality of speaking	**.80**	.20	.21
12. Careless work completion	.15	**.72**	.36
13. Time to complete work	.36	.21	**.61**
14. Attention without prompts	.24	.35	**.53**
15. Requires assistance	.44	.39	**.53**
16. Begins work carelessly	.16	.82	.02
17. Recall difficulties	**.66**	.35	.38
18. Stare excessively	.19	.39	**.67**
19. Social withdrawal	.16	.28	**.57**
Estimate of % variance	55.5	6.6	6.1

Note: Boldface values indicate items included in the factor named in the column head.

*From "Teacher Ratings of Academic Skills: The Development of the Academic Performance Rating Scale," by G. J. DuPaul, M. D. Rapport, and L. M. Perriello, 1991, *School Psychology Review, 20*, p. 290. Copyright 1991 by National Association of School Psychologists. Reprinted by permission.

TABLE 2 Means and Standard Deviations for the APRS by Grade and Gender*

Grade	Total score	Academic Success	Impulse Control	Academic Productivity
Grade 1 (*n* = 82)				
Girls (*n* = 40)	67.02 (16.27)	23.92 (7.37)	9.76 (2.49)	44.68 (10.91)
Boys (*n* = 42)	71.95 (16.09)	26.86 (6.18)	10.67 (2.82)	46.48 (11.24)
Grade 2 (*n* = 91)				
Girls (*n* = 46)	72.56 (12.33)	26.61 (5.55)	10.15 (2.70)	47.85 (7.82)
Boys (*n* = 45)	67.84 (14.86)	25.24 (6.15)	9.56 (2.72)	44.30 (10.76)
Grade 3 (*n* = 92)				
Girls (*n* = 46)	72.10 (14.43)	25.07 (6.07)	10.86 (2.65)	47.88 (9.35)
Boys (*n* = 49)	68.49 (16.96)	25.26 (6.53)	9.27 (2.67)	45.61 (11.89)
Grade 4 (*n* = 79)				
Girls (*n* = 38)	67.79 (18.69)	24.08 (7.56)	10.36 (2.91)	44.26 (11.96)
Boys (*n* = 41)	69.77 (15.83)	25.35 (6.50)	9.83 (2.77)	45.71 (10.22)
Grade 5 (*n* = 79)				
Girls (*n* = 44)	73.02 (14.10)	26.11 (6.01)	10.76 (2.34)	48.36 (9.05)
Boys (*n* = 35)	63.68 (18.04)	23.14 (7.31)	8.69 (2.82)	42.40 (12.47)
Grade 6 (*n* = 70)				
Girls (*n* = 31)	74.10 (14.45)	26.59 (6.26)	10.79 (2.25)	48.77 (9.13)
Boys (*n* = 39)	65.24 (12.39)	23.75 (5.90)	9.05 (2.35)	43.59 (8.19)

Note: Standard deviations are in parentheses.

*From "Teacher Ratings of Academic Skills: The Development of the Academic Performance Rating Scale," by G. J. DuPaul, M. D. Rapport, and L. M. Perriello, 1991, *School Psychology Review, 20*, p. 291. Copyright 1991 by National Association of School Psychologists. Reprinted by permission.

♦♦♦

Student Interview

♦

It is important in the process of academic assessment to determine how the student being assessed perceives the demands of the academic environment. This information is best obtained through an interview of the student. Specifically, questions should cover the following: the degree to which the student understands the directions of assignments; the degree of success predicted by the student on each assignment; the student's perception of how much time he/she is given by the teacher to complete assignments; the student's knowledge of how to seek assistance when experiencing difficulty; and the student's understanding of the consequences of not completing academic work. This information can be obtained by means of a semistructured interview, conducted immediately after an observation of the student engaged in an assigned task. Two forms are provided for conducting these interviews. The first is from The Instructional Environment Scale (TIES; Ysseldyke & Christenson, 1987). The second form consists of more general guidelines that can be used to interview a student.

TIES STUDENT INTERVIEW*

1. I want you to tell me what you needed to do on these assignments.

a. What did your teacher want you to learn?

b. What did your teacher tell you about why these assignments are important?

c. What did you have to do?

d. Show me how you did the work. (Have student explain a sample item.)

2. I am going to ask you several questions. In each case, I want you to tell me your answer by using this scale, where 1 means "not very much" and 4 means "very much."

a. Sometimes students understantd their assignments. Sometimes they don't. Show me how well you understand the assignment. 1 2 3 4

b. How much did you believe you could do the assignment? 1 2 3 4

c. How interesting is this work for you? 1 2 3 4

3. Now I have some other questions.

a. Sometimes students cannot finish their work, and sometimes they have extra time. How much time do you usually get to finish your work: too little (1), just about right (2), or too much (3)? 1 2 3

b. Does your teacher call on you to answer questions in class: never (1), not much (2), a lot (3)? 1 2 3

4. What does your teacher expect you to do when he or she gives these assignments:

a. If you are confused?

b. If you are done with your work?

5. What does your teacher tell you about:

a. Completing your work? (What happens if your work is not done?)

b. Getting the answers correct? (What happens if you make mistakes?)

c. Having neat papers? (What happens if your work is messy?)

6. Student Success Rate:

a. Number of questions completed ____________________

b. Number of correct answers ____________________

c. Total number of questions assigned ____________________

d. Success rate ____________________

e. Kind of errors made by the student ____________________

____

*From *TIES: The Instructional Environment Scale* by J. Ysseldyke and S. Christenson. Austin, TX: Pro-Ed. Copyright 1987 by J. Ysseldyke and S. Christenson. Reprinted by permission.

STUDENT INTERVIEW

Student Name ______________________________

Subject ______________________________

Date ______________________________

STUDENT-REPORTED BEHAVIOR ____ None completed for this area

Understands expectations of teacher	☐ Yes	☐ No	☐ Not sure
Understands assignments	☐ Yes	☐ No	☐ Not sure
Feels he/she can do the assignments	☐ Yes	☐ No	☐ Not sure
Likes the subject	☐ Yes	☐ No	☐ Not sure
Feels he/she is given enough time to complete assignments	☐ Yes	☐ No	☐ Not sure
Feels he/she is called upon to participate in discussions	☐ Yes	☐ No	☐ Not sure

General comments:

Questions used to guide interview:

Do you think you are pretty good in ________________?

If you had to pick one thing about ______________ you like, what would it be?

If you had to pick one thing about ______________ you don't like, what would it be?

What do you do when you are unable to solve a problem or answer a question with your assignment in ______________?

Do you enjoy working with other students when you are having trouble with your assignment in ________________?

Does the teacher call on you too often? Not often enough? In ________________?

*Direct Observation: Manual for the Behavioral Observation of Students in Schools (B.O.S.S.)**

Systematically observing students in classrooms is an essential part of the assessment of the academic environment. This is true whether the referral problem is not completing assignments, having difficulty in reading, or being unable to add quickly and accurately.

Although learning to conduct systematic observations is not difficult, it does take some concentrated practice and effort to master the method. It is a rare person (if such a person exists) who can put on a pair of skis for the first time and go schussing down the slopes of Killington. It is a rare person who can pick up a basketball and make four consecutive 3-pointers. It is a rare person who can sit down at a piano for the first time and play popular songs. It is a rare person who can get in front of a group of third-grade children and teach subtraction with regrouping. Acquiring the skills to be a good skier, a good athlete, a good pianist, or a good teacher takes practice. Learning these skills calls for studying persons who are considered experts at the skills in question, trying out the new skills under the supervision of such experts, receiving feedback regarding one's performance, and then practicing the newly learned skills.

This manual describes the rationale and process of direct observation. In particular, the use of the B.O.S.S., a measure designed specifically for direct observation of academic skills, is presented.

*Many thanks to Mark Fugate, Ph.D., for suggestions and contributions to the development of this section of the workbook.

RATIONALE

Systematic direct observation is defined as a form of quantitative data collection. Its main purpose is numerical recording of the behaviors occurring in the observational setting. For example, if Roberta is reported as not paying attention, systematic observation may show that she was off-task 50% of the time. If Jason is reported as not completing his work, systematic observation may find that, on the average, Jason completes only two of five in-class math assignments per day. If Miguel is reported as fighting on the playground at recess, systematic observation may reveal he was sent to the principal for fighting five times in the past two weeks. In each case, the use of systematic observation attempts to capture quantitatively the behavior actually taking place.

Of course, teachers and other professionals are constantly observing children in schools; this form of observation provides a subjective impression of a child's behavior. These impressions are important and meaningful, and can be viewed as helpful in making sense of a child's classroom behavior. Unfortunately, although these subjective impressions are frequently accurate, they can also be inaccurate. For example, Marcus may be reported by a teacher to be a disruptive and "nasty" child because of his frequent teasing of peers. Such a report suggests that the behavior occurs frequently and should be easily observable. If the teacher is asked to complete a rating scale that includes items about teasing, the teacher may report that the behavior occurs often, when in reality the behavior may occur rarely. However, the fact that the behavior is viewed as negative and obnoxious by the teacher may make it seem as if it is much worse than it really is. Using a form of systematic observation makes it possible to describe the teasing objectively in terms of its frequency. Of course, even a low frequency of misbehavior can be very troubling; teasing that occurs once per week may be viewed as out of line and as needing to be stopped. However, knowing that the problem is not as severe as was first thought may be very important in deciding how best to remediate it.

There are four important reasons for conducting systematic observations. First, as already noted, getting subjective opinions about behavior is important, because these perceptions represent how important persons who deal with the problem see it; indeed, they form the basis of what these persons think is going on. However, subjective perceptions need to be systematically confirmed or disconfirmed. In addition, as suggested above, the problem may be either less or more severe than originally indicated. Thus, two important reasons for conducting systematic observation are the need to confirm or disconfirm subjective reports and to determine the exact severity of the reported problem.

A third important reason for conducting systematic observation is to provide a baseline or benchmark against which to assess the success or failure of an instructional intervention. Whenever changes in behavior occur, it is important to document the relative impact of the intervention by comparing the student's present performance with his/her performance prior to the intervention. This allows the teacher, the student, and the parents to see the gains (or losses) in performance that have occurred over time. It is also required in some states (e.g., Pennsylvania, Iowa) that such baseline data be obtained as part of the evaluation process.

A final reason to collect systematic observation data is to provide feedback to all parties (parents, students, teachers, and other school professionals) regarding the types and levels of problems students are currently having. By using systematic observation, interested persons can actually see how behavior is changing in the classroom.

DEFINING THE BEHAVIORS FOR OBSERVATION

Systematic observation requires that the behaviors to be observed be carefully and precisely defined. Behaviors that are defined too broadly may be difficult to observe accurately. At the same time, behaviors defined too narrowly may not be meaningful units of responding. The key to effectively defining behaviors for observation is to think about which ones are likely to be most relevant to the problem(s) of interest in the classroom.

When the problem is in the area of academics, the literature has suggested that the observation of student academic engaged time is a critical variable. Strong and significant relationships have been identified between high levels of academic engagement and successful academic performance. This suggests a need for a careful analysis of the types of engagement and nonengagement that a student exhibits in the classroom (see Chapter 2 of Shapiro, 1996, for a more detailed discussion).

The B.O.S.S. includes two categories of engagement and three categories of nonengagement. An additional category that examines the types of instruction occurring in the classroom is also included in the code. When the interaction of the student's engaged and nonengaged time is examined, a clear picture of the student's behavior in a context of meaningful academic outcomes can be obtained.

GETTING STARTED

Materials

Two sharp pencils or fine-point pens.
Clipboard.
Coding interval audiotape with a tape player and earpiece (or headphones). A stopwatch is not recommended, since it can be difficult to attend both to the watch and to events in the classroom. In addition, keeping track of the interval in which the observation is taking place is critical. Use of an audio cuing device allows the observer to maintain vigilance to the classroom while simultaneously recording with accuracy.
B.O.S.S. coding sheet(s) permitting up to 30 minutes of observation. Each minute is divided into four intervals of 15 seconds each. An observation sheet is provided for use with the B.O.S.S., consisting of 180 intervals per page (45 minutes).

Classroom Manners

Before observing in a classroom, the observer will need to become familiar with the daily schedule, class routine, and physical layout of the classroom.
The observer should meet briefly with the teacher before the observation, to learn about classroom rules or procedures that may be in effect during the observation.

The observer should ask the teacher where the best place to sit or stand will be so as to directly observe the target student.
The observer needs to have a clear view of the student, but should not be too obtrusive and should be sure to stay out of major traffic areas for other students.
During the observation, the teacher should teach as he/she normally does.
The observer should minimize any interactions with students or the teacher during the observation period.
The teacher should not introduce the observer to the class when he/she arrives, but should be instructed to tell the students (prior to your arrival) that someone will be coming to observe what goes on in the classroom.
If the assessment will include working individually with the target student, it is recommended that the direct observations be conducted before the observer meets individually with the student.
The observer's entrance into the classroom should be as naturalistic as possible. It can help if he/she enters the classroom during a natural break in the instructional routine.

MAKING A CODING INTERVAL AUDIOTAPE

Making an audiotape to use for cuing during observations is not difficult, but does take a little time. There are two approaches to making a tape. Regardless of the method used, a cuing tape for the B.O.S.S. should be at least 30 minutes in length and contain intervals of 15 seconds.

Method 1: Talking a Tape

The first method is to generate a tape recording by talking the intervals aloud. Using a stopwatch and a tape recorder, the observer simply states the necessary intervals. Each interval is cued by saying, "Observe 1," "Observe 2," "Observe 3," and so forth as each interval passes. Using the word "Observe" before each number is said provides a cue that signals when the interval is about to begin. A brief statement should also be provide prior to beginning the first observation interval, such as "Get ready to observe." As the last interval on the tape ends, the observer should record an ending statement, such as "End of observation" or some other appropriate closing comment.

An advantage of talking the intervals is that it provides a cue immediately before each momentary time sample observation must be made. Preparing the tape can be tedious, and if concentration is not maintained, accuracy of the tape may be compromised (i.e., each interval may not be 15 seconds in length).

Method 2: Using Computer-Generated Tones

Another method for making an audiotape for cuing intervals is to use a tape that makes a tone at every change of intervals. This type of tape is more accurate than a talking tape, and producing it is less tedious. However, such a tape does not contain any cues as to the specific interval in which the observer is collecting data. Turco and Shear (1991) have provided a computer program that can be written to cue the tape. To use this method for generating a tape, the tape recorder microphone should be placed near the computer's external speaker, and the following program written in the QBASIC language should be run:

```
10  INPUT "HOW MANY SECONDS BETWEEN BEEPS";S
20  INPUT "HOW MANY MINUTES";M
30  Q = (M*60)/S:C = 0:BEEP: BEEP: BEEP
40  TIMER ON: ON TIMER(S) GOSUB 80
50  DO WHILE INKEY$ = "": if C> = Q THEN GOTO 90
70  LOOP
80  BEEP: C = C+ 1: RETURN
90  BEEP: BEEP: END
```

When the program is entered and run, the computer will prompt the user when to enter the number of seconds in each interval and the number of minutes in the observation session.

COMPLETING IDENTIFYING INFORMATION

The coding sheet used with the B.O.S.S. is included at the end of this section of the workbook. At the top of the B.O.S.S. coding sheet, the observer should be sure to write in the child's name, date, his/her own name, and the subject matter being observed. In addition, the observer is asked to note the type of instructional setting observed:

ISW:TPsnt (Student in Independent Seatwork, Teacher Present)
In this setting, the student is doing independent seatwork while the teacher is available to assist individual children. Typically, the teacher is circulating around the room.

ISW:TSmGp (Student in Independent Seatwork, Teacher in Small Group not Including Target Student)
This setting is marked when the target student is engaged in independent seatwork and the teacher is working with a small group that *does not* include the target student.

SmGp:TPsnt (Student in Small Group Led by Teacher)
This setting is marked when the target student is in a small group (defined as eight or fewer students) that is led by the teacher.

LgGp:TPsnt (Student in Large Group Led by Teacher)
This setting is marked when the target student is in a large group (defined as more than 8 students) that is led by the teacher.

Other

When "Other" is used, the type of instructional setting should be noted in the margin.

The classroom setting is marked by circling the appropriate designation. If the instructional activity changes during the course of the observation, this change should be noted on the observation form by circling the interval where the change occurred and writing in the type of setting that is now in place.

OBSERVING PEER COMPARISON STUDENTS

A behavioral observation is more meaningful if the target student's behavior is compared to the same behavior displayed by peers. The B.O.S.S. requires that data be collected not only on the target student but also on peers in the same classroom. As noted on the B.O.S.S. observation form, every fifth interval is shaded. During each of these intervals, observations are conducted on a randomly selected peer rather than the target student. Before beginning the observation, the observer should decide the sequence of peer comparison observations. For example, the observer may decide to start in the front left of the classroom and observe a different peer each fifth interval, moving down the row and then from back to front. In truth, it does not matter in which order the peer comparison data are collected. It does help, however, for the observer to have an observation plan in mind before beginning the observation of the target student.

Data from intervals in which different peers were observed are combined to derive a peer comparison score for each of the behaviors.

CODING ACADEMIC ENGAGEMENT

The B.O.S.S. divides academic engagement into two subcategories: active or passive engaged time. In either case, the student is considered to be on-task. Each of these behaviors is recorded as a momentary time sample. At the beginning of each cued interval, the observer looks at the targeted student: determines whether the student is on-task; and, if so, whether the on-task behavior constitutes an active or passive form of engagement as defined below. The occurrence of the behavior at that moment is recorded by making a mark in the appropriate box on the scoring sheet.

Active Engaged Time (AET)

Active engaged time (AET) is defined as those times when the student is actively attending to the assigned work. Examples of AET include:

Writing
Reading aloud

Raising a hand
Talking to the teacher about the assigned material
Talking to a peer about the assigned material
Looking up a word in a dictionary

AET *should not* be scored if the student is:

Talking about nonacademic material (verbal off-task)
Walking to the worksheet bin (motor off-task)
Calling out (verbal off-task) unless it is considered an appropriate response style for that classroom
Aimlessly flipping the pages of a book (motor off-task)
Engaging in any other form of off-task behavior

Passive Engaged Time (PET)

Passive engaged time (PET) is defined as those times when the student is passively attending to assigned work. Examples of PET include:

Listening to a lecture
Looking at an academic worksheet
Silently reading assigned material
Looking at the blackboard during teacher instruction
Listening to a peer respond to a question

PET *should not* be scored if the student is:

Aimlessly looking around the classroom (passive off-task)
Silently reading unassigned material (passive off-task)
Engaging in any other form of off-task behavior

At times it may be difficult to determine immediately whether a child is passively engaged or daydreaming at the first moment of an interval. In this case, it is appropriate to code PET if it becomes apparent later during that interval that the student was indeed passively engaged.

CODING NONENGAGEMENT

When a student is not engaged in academic behavior, three possible categories of off-task behavior are coded. These behaviors are recorded by means of a partial interval observation method: If any of the three behaviors occurs at any point during the interval, a mark is made in the appropriate box. Multiple occurrences of the same behavior within a single interval are noted only once.

Off-Task Motor (OFT-M)

Off-task motor behaviors (OFT-M) are defined as any instance of motor activity that are not directly associated with an assigned academic task. Examples of OFT-M include:

Engaging in any out-of-seat behavior (defined as buttocks not in contact with the seat)
Aimlessly flipping the pages of a book
Manipulating objects not related to the academic task (e.g., playing with a paper clip, throwing paper, twirling a pencil, folding paper)
Physically touching another student when not related to an academic task
Bending or reaching, such as picking up a pencil on the floor
Drawing or writing not related to an assigned academic activity
Turning around in seat, oriented away from the classroom instruction
Fidgeting in seat (i.e., engaging in repetitive motor movements for at least 3 consecutive seconds; student must be off-task for this category to be scored)

OFT-M *should not* be scored if the student is:

Passing paper to a student as instructed by the teacher
Coloring on an assigned worksheet as instructed (AET)
Laughing at a joke told by another student (off-task verbal)
Swinging feet while working on assigned material (AET or PET)

Off-Task Verbal (OFT-V)

Off-task verbal behaviors (OFT-V) are defined as any audible verbalizations that are not permitted and/or are not related to an assigned academic task. Examples of OFT-V include:

Making any audible sound, such as whistling, humming, forced burping
Talking to another student about issues unrelated to an assigned academic task
Talking to another student about an assigned academic task when such talk is prohibited by the teacher
Making unauthorized comments or remarks
Calling out answers to academic problems when the teacher has not specifically asked for an answer or permitted such behavior

OFT-V *should not* be scored if the student is:

Laughing at a joke told by the teacher
Talking to another student about the assigned academic work during a cooperative learning group (AET)
Calling out the answer to a problem when the teacher has permitted such behavior during instruction (AET)

Off-Task Passive (OFT-P)

Off-task passive behaviors (OFT-P) are defined as those times when a student is passively not attending to an assigned academic activity for a period of at least 3 consecutive seconds. Included are those times when a student is quietly waiting after the completion of an assigned task, but is not engaged in an activity authorized by the teacher. Examples of OFT-P behavior include:

Sitting quietly in an unassigned activity
Looking around the room
Staring out the window
Passively listening to other students talk about issues unrelated to the assigned academic activity

It is important to note that the student must be passively off-task for 3 consecutive seconds *within an interval* to be scored. Should the interval end before the full 3-second period occurs, OFT-P is not scored for that interval, and a new consecutive 3-second period is required for the next interval. For instance, suppose a student begins to stare out the window during the third interval of observation. The observer counts only 2 seconds before the fourth interval begins. The student continues to stare out the window for over 3 seconds in this interval. In this case, only the fourth interval should be scored for OFT-P. If the student had stopped staring out the window after 2 seconds of the fourth interval, than OFT-P *should not* have been scored for either interval. In addition, OFT-P *should not* be scored if the student is:

Quietly reading an assigned book (PET)
Passively listening to other students talk about the assigned work in a cooperative learning group (PET)

CODING TEACHER-DIRECTED INSTRUCTION (TDI)

Teacher-directed instruction (TDI) is coded every fifth interval, again by means of a partial interval observation method. The purpose of these observations is to provide a sampling of time in which the teacher is actively engaged in directed instruction of the classroom. TDI is defined as those times when the teacher is directly instructing the class or individuals within the class. Examples of TDI include times when the teacher is:

Instructing the whole class or group
Demonstrating academic material at the blackboard
Individually assisting a student with an assigned task

TDI *should not* be scored if the teacher is:

Scolding the class or an individual student for misbehavior
Giving instructions for an academic activity

Sitting at his/her desk grading papers
Speaking to an individual student or the class about nonacademic issues

REVIEW: PROCEDURE FOR CONDUCTING THE OBSERVATION

After the observer is seated in the classroom, he/she begins the observation by starting the audiotape. The observer is cued with the words "Observe 1." Using the number word as the indicator of the beginning of each interval, the observer immediately records at the moment when "1" is heard whether the student is actively or passively engaged in academic behavior. If the student is off-task at the moment when "1" is heard, the observer leaves the boxes blank. For the remainder of the interval, the observer watches the student to see whether he/she engages in any form of off-task behavior. Before the next interval begins, if the student gets out of his/her seat and then talks to another student about nonacademic issues, marks should be made in the OFT-M and OFT-V columns of interval 1. The process is repeated until the observer reaches interval 5. Having decided to start with the students in the first row of desks for purposes of peer comparison data collection, the observer, upon hearing the words "Observe 5," now looks to see whether the student sitting in the first seat in the first row is on-task. That student is now observed for any off-task behavior throughout the remainder of the interval. In addition, during the 5th interval, the observer records whether the teacher engaged in any directed instruction. When the 6th interval begins, the observer returns to watching and recording the behavior of the target student. This process is repeated until the observation is completed. Figure 3 displays a completed sample observation using the B.O.S.S.

B.O.S.S.

Behavioral Observation of Students in Schools

Child Observed: __Justin_______ **Academic Subject:** _____Math____
Date: __ 9/15/95______ **Setting:** ISW:TPsnt SmGp:TPsnt ✓
Observer: ___JGL _______ ISW:TSmGp LgGp:TPsnt
Time of Observation ___10:30 AM____ Other: ______________

Moment	1	2	3	4	5*	6	7	8	9	10*	11	12	13	14	15*	S	P	T
AET	\		\		\	\	\			\		\				5	2	
PET		\						\	\		\			\	\	5	1	
Partial																		
OFT-M	\								\						\	2	1	
OFT-V						\	\			\	\					3	1	
OFT-P	\			\	\								\			3	1	
TDI															\			1

Moment	16	17	18	19	20*	21	22	23	24	25*	26	27	28	29	30*	S	P	T
AET	\			\							\				\	3	1	
PET			\		\	\					\	\				4	1	
Partial																		
OFT-M		\														1	0	
OFT-V		\								\						1	1	
OFT-P							\	\	\				\	\		5	0	
TDI					\					\					\			3

Moment	31	32	33	34	35*	36	37	38	39	40*	41	42	43	44	45*	S	P	T
AET		\			\											1	1	
PET	\		\	\							\	\	\	\		7	0	
Partial																		
OFT-M								\	\						\	2	1	
OFT-V						\	\									2	0	
OFT-P										\						0	1	
TDI										\					\			2

Moment	46	47	48	49	50*	51	52	53	54	55*	56	57	58	59	60*	S	P	T
AET					\											0	1	
PET		\	\	\						\					\	3	2	
Partial																		
OFT-M											\					1	0	
OFT-V											\	\				2	0	
OFT-P						\	\	\	\					\		5	0	
TDI															\			1

	Target Student				*Peer Comparison				Teacher	
Total Intervals Observed __48__	S AET	_9_	% AET	_18.8_	S AET	_5_	% AET	_41.7_	S TDI	__7_
	S PET	19_	% PET	_40.0_	S PET	_4_	% PET	_33.3_	% TDI	_58.3_
	S OFT-M	_6_	% OFT-M	_12.5_	S OFT-M	_2_	% OFT-M	_16.7_	Total Intervals Observed	__12__
	S OFT-V	_8_	% OFT-V	_16.7_	S OFT-V	_2_	% OFT-V	_16.7_		
	S OFT-P	13_	% OFT-P	_27.1_	S OFT-P	_2_	% OFT-P	_16.7_		

FIGURE 3. Completed B.O.S.S. observation on Justin.

SCORING THE B.O.S.S.

All categories of the B.O.S.S. are scored using the same metric: percentage of intervals in which the behavior occurred. Scoring requires that the number of intervals in which the behavior was marked as occurring be divided by the total number of intervals of observing the student, and that this result be multiplied by 100.

Step 1: Add the number of times each behavior occurred for the target student *only*, across the rows. Enter this number on the data collection sheet in the corresponding cell under the column marked "S" (for target student). Be sure *not* to add the number of occurrences in the intervals where peer comparison data were collected (see Figure 4).

As can be seen in Figure 4, the target student was observed to have engaged in AET for 5 intervals out of the first 15 observed, PET for 5, OFT-M for 2, OFT-V for 3, and OFT-P for 3.

Step 2: Add up the number of intervals each behavior is observed for the target student across the entire observation, and record the total in the lower left portion of the form. This is done by simply adding the "S" row totals for each behavior.

As can be seen in Figure 3, the target student was found to engage in AET for 9 intervals, PET for 19 intervals, OFT-M for 6 intervals, OFT-V for 8 intervals, and OFT-P for 13 intervals.

Step 3: Determine the total number of intervals in which the target student was observed, and record this number in the space provided in the lower left portion of the data collection sheet. Again, be sure to eliminate any intervals in which the peer comparison data were collected.

As is evident in Figure 3, the target student was observed for a total of 48 intervals during this observation.

Step 4: Divide the number of occurrences of each behavior by the total intervals observed, and multiply by 100. This is the percentage of intervals in which the behavior was observed to occur. Record this in the spaces provided.

Step 5: Repeat this process, but now calculate only the intervals in which peer comparison data (P) were collected. Eliminate any intervals where the target student was observed (see Figure 5).

Step 6: Repeat the process one more time, but now examine only the intervals in which TDI data were collected (see Figure 6). Eliminate any intervals in which the target student data were collected. Note that

Moment	1	2	3	4	5*	6	7	8	9	10*	11	12	13	14	15	S	P	T
AET	\		\		\	\	\			\		\				5		
PET		\						\	\		\			\	\	5		
Partial																		
OFT-M	\								\						\	2		
OFT-V						\	\			\	\					3		
OFT-P	\			\	\								\			3		
TDI					\										\			

FIGURE 4. First 15 intervals of B.O.S.S. observation for Justin.

Moment	1	2	3	4	5*	6	7	8	9	10*	11	12	13	14	15	S	P	T
AET	\		\		\	\	\			\		\				5	2	
PET		\						\	\		\			\	\	5	1	
Partial																		
OFT-M	\								\						\	2	1	
OFT-V						\	\			\	\					3	1	
OFT-P	\			\	\								\			3	1	
TDI					\										\			

FIGURE 5. First 15 intervals of B.O.S.S. observation for Justin scored for peer comparison students.

Moment	1	2	3	4	5*	6	7	8	9	10*	11	12	13	14	15	S	P	T
AET	\		\		\	\	\			\		\				5	2	
PET		\						\	\		\			\	\	5	1	
Partial																		
OFT-M	\								\						\	2	1	
OFT-V						\	\			\	\					3	1	
OFT-P	\			\	\								\			3	1	
TDI					\										\			2

FIGURE 6. First 15 intervals of B.O.S.S. observation for Justin scored for TDI.

the intervals in which peer comparison data were collected are the same ones in which TDI is observed.

In the example shown in Figure 3, the target student was observed for a total of 48 intervals, and peers for 12 intervals. Across the observation, AET for the target student was observed 9 times, or 18.8% of the 48 intervals. For the peer comparison students, AET was observed 5 times, or 41.7% of the 12 intervals. Calculations for all categories should result in the summary on the bottom of Figure 3.

INTERPRETATION OF B.O.S.S. DATA

Interpretation of the B.O.S.S. can involve analysis of several aspects of classroom behavior. First, the B.O.S.S. shows the levels of academic engagement and nonengagement for the targeted student in the particular setting of observation. By comparing the combined percentages of AET and PET against those of the three OFT categories, the observer can establish the amounts of a student's on- and off-task behavior. These data can provide the observer with information about the extent to which the target student is effectively engaged in the learning process.

Second, observations across multiple settings make it possible to determine, relative differences among the target student's levels of academic engagement in different instructional environments. For example, it may be found that a student has much higher levels of on-task behavior when he/she is in a teacher-led setting than when he/she is involved in independent seatwork.

Third, by examining the relative differences between AET and PET, the observer can determine whether the opportunities to respond (AET level) for a student are high enough to provide clear evidence of academic progress. Students who are struggling in school are often found to have relatively low levels of AET even when they are on-task.

Fourth, and most importantly, the observer can compare the performance of the target student against that of the student's peers. Use of this type of local normative data is crucial in understanding the degree to which the levels of behavior obtained for the target student differ from the expected performance of the student's classmates. At times, a student who appears to have a very low level of on-task behavior may be found to have a level equivalent to those of his/her peers, suggesting that the student's behavior may not be beyond the expectations set by the classroom teacher. On the other hand, a student appearing to have a very high level of on-task behavioral performance may be viewed as not meeting classroom expectations. When comparisons are made to the student's peers, it may become evident that although the student's level is high, it is significantly lower than the levels of his/her peers.

One of the most frequently asked questions related to conducting systematic observation is "How much observation is needed?" The answer is "It depends." Accurate observations require at least 10–15 minutes. Optimally, observations should be 20–30 minutes each. In the best of all possible worlds, the observation should be repeated over 2–3 days, and possibly across different types of academic settings (e.g., independent work in reading, small-group activities in math, large-group activities in science, etc.). Obviously, the practical restrictions of time may limit how much observation can be done. So the question is whether a single observation can be enough.

The key to good observation is that it accurately represents the child's behavior at the time of the observation and at other times of the day. If a child's behavior tends to be highly variable from day to day or hour to hour, a single observation at one time in one setting may not be sufficient. Likewise, if a child's behavior changes because there is an observer in the classroom or the child is having a "good day," a single observation may not be enough. Certainly, some degree of stable responding from day to day is important; however, the problem of some children is precisely that they are inconsistent, so expecting consistency in those cases is unrealistic.

One way to address this problem is always to ask the teacher whether the behavior seen that day was typical of the student's performance. If it was, then the observation may be enough. However, if the behavior was atypical of what the teacher thinks is the student's usual behavior, then additional observations are needed.

Another important issue to consider in deciding whether enough observation has been done is whether or not the situation in which the behavior was observed represents where the problems tend to occur. For example, although the teacher notes that Josh has problems during independent seatwork activities, an important question for the teacher is whether there are equal problems in math and reading. One hypothesis about Josh's behavior may be that his skill levels differ across subject matter and the differential skill levels result in differential behavioral outcomes. Thus, it may be crucial to conduct observations during independent seatwork periods in both a math and a reading activity.

The general rule of thumb often recommended is that observers should plan to conduct at least three observations. If behavior is consistent after two observations, then the third can perhaps be bypassed. If the behavior is not consistent after three observations, then at least one additional observation should be conducted. It is important to note that the decision about when enough observation has been conducted must be a clinical decision based on sound clinical judgment. There is no single rule that can be applied in all cases.

In the example shown in Figure 3, the student, Justin, was observed during his math class. Throughout the observation, the teacher was engaged in teaching a small group (6 students) in which Justin was included. Peer comparison data for this observation were collected among the other 5 students in Justin's small group. The observation lasted for 10 minutes and was conducted at 10:30 A.M. Justin's overall level of on-task behavior was much lower than that of his peers. In total, Justin was academically engaged for 58.8% of the observed intervals, whereas his peers remained engaged for 75.0% of the observed intervals. In addition, when Justin was engaged, he spent the largest proportion of his time (40.0% of the intervals) in passive rather than active forms of engagement. In contrast, his peers were actively engaged for 41.7% of the intervals.

When Justin was off-task, he was primarily nonengaged in passive ways. Typically, this involved looking away from his work and staring out the windows. Justin was also off-task through getting out of his seat, as well as speaking to his peers. However, these off-task behaviors for Justin were comparable to those of his classmates.

Throughout the observation, Justin's teacher was engaged in directed teaching activities for approximately 58.3% of the observed intervals. During intervals when Justin's teacher was not instructing the class, she was observed in classroom management activities, such as redirecting Justin and other students to pay attention to her direction.

In regard to interpreting data from the B.O.S.S., it is important to note that the observer does not view the level of behavior obtained through the observation to represent an estimate of the amount of time that a behavior would occur. Because the observation system is derived from a time-sampling strategy, it would be inaccurate to say that the behavior actually occurred for __% of the time. This is especially true since partial interval recording systems (such as those used here for the off-task behaviors and TDI) are likely to overestimate the actual rate of a behavior's occurrence. It is also important to note that the data collected for the target student are likely to be more reliable and stable then the data collected for peer comparison purposes. The more observation intervals, the better the stability of the measure. In this observation example, there were 48 observations of the target student and only 12 of the peers. Data collected on peers must be considered cautiously in the interpretation of results.

B.O.S.S.

Behavioral Observation of Students in Schools

Child Observed: ____________
Date: ____________
Observer: ____________
Time of Observation ____________

Academic Subject: ____________
Setting: ISW:TPsnt SmGp:TPsnt
ISW:TSmGp LgGp:TPsnt
Other: ____________

Moment	121	122	123	124	125*	126	127	128	129	130*	131	132	133	134	135*	S	P	T
AET																		
PET																		
Partial																		
OFT-M																		
OFT-V																		
OFT-P																		
TDI																		

Moment	136	137	138	139	140*	141	142	143	144	145*	146	147	148	149	150*	S	P	T
AET																		
PET																		
Partial																		
OFT-M																		
OFT-V																		
OFT-P																		
TDI																		

Moment	151	152	153	154	155*	156	157	158	159	160*	161	162	163	164	165*	S	P	T
AET																		
PET																		
Partial																		
OFT-M																		
OFT-V																		
OFT-P																		
TDI																		

Moment	166	167	168	169	170*	171	172	173	174	175*	176	177	178	179	180*	S	P	T
AET																		
PET																		
Partial																		
OFT-M																		
OFT-V																		
OFT-P																		
TDI																		

Total Intervals Observed ____

Target Student

S AET ___	% AET	____
S PET ___	% PET	____
S OFT-M ___	% OFT-M	____
S OFT-V ___	% OFT-V	____
S OFT-P ___	% OFT-P	____

***Peer Comparison**

S AET ___	% AET	____
S PET ___	% PET	____
S OFT-M ___	% OFT-M	____
S OFT-V ___	% OFT-V	____
S OFT-P ___	% OFT-P	____

Teacher
S TDI ____
% TDI ____
Total Intervals Observed
____

B.O.S.S.

Behavioral Observation of Students in Schools

Child Observed: ____________
Date: ____________
Observer: ____________
Time of Observation: ____________

Academic Subject: ____________
Setting: ISW:TPsnt SmGp:TPsnt ISW:TSmGp LgGp:TPsnt Other: ____________

Moment	61	62	63	64	65*	66	67	68	69	70*	71	72	73	74	75*	S	P	T
AET																		
PET																		
Partial																		
OFT-M																		
OFT-V																		
OFT-P																		
TDI																		

Moment	76	77	78	79	80*	81	82	83	84	85*	86	87	88	89	90*	S	P	T
AET																		
PET																		
Partial																		
OFT-M																		
OFT-V																		
OFT-P																		
TDI																		

Moment	91	92	93	94	95*	96	97	98	99	100*	101	102	103	104	105*	S	P	T
AET																		
PET																		
Partial																		
OFT-M																		
OFT-V																		
OFT-P																		
TDI																		

Moment	106	107	108	109	110*	111	112	113	114	115*	116	117	118	119	120*	S	P	T
AET																		
PET																		
Partial																		
OFT-M																		
OFT-V																		
OFT-P																		
TDI																		

Total Intervals Observed ____

Target Student

S AET	___	% AET	___
S PET	___	% PET	___
S OFT-M	___	% OFT-M	___
S OFT-V	___	% OFT-V	___
S OFT-P	___	% OFT-P	___

***Peer Comparison**

S AET	___	% AET	___
S PET	___	% PET	___
S OFT-M	___	% OFT-M	___
S OFT-V	___	% OFT-V	___
S OFT-P	___	% OFT-P	___

Teacher

S TDI ___
% TDI ___
Total Intervals Observed ____

B.O.S.S.

Behavioral Observation of Students in Schools

Child Observed: ______________
Date: ______________
Observer: ______________
Time of Observation ______________

Academic Subject: ____________
Setting: ISW:TPsnt SmGp:TPsnt
ISW:TSmGp LgGp:TPsnt
Other: _________________

Moment	1	2	3	4	5*	6	7	8	9	10*	11	12	13	14	15*	S	P	T
AET																		
PET																		
Partial																		
OFT-M																		
OFT-V																		
OFT-P																		
TDI																		

Moment	16	17	18	19	20*	21	22	23	24	25*	26	27	28	29	30*	S	P	T
AET																		
PET																		
Partial																		
OFT-M																		
OFT-V																		
OFT-P																		
TDI																		

Moment	31	32	33	34	35*	36	37	38	39	40*	41	42	43	44	45*	S	P	T
AET																		
PET																		
Partial																		
OFT-M																		
OFT-V																		
OFT-P																		
TDI																		

Moment	46	47	48	49	50*	51	52	53	54	55*	56	57	58	59	60*	S	P	T
AET																		
PET																		
Partial																		
OFT-M																		
OFT-V																		
OFT-P																		
TDI																		

Total Intervals Observed ______

Target Student

S AET ___ % AET ____
S PET ___ % PET ____
S OFT-M ___ % OFT-M ____
S OFT-V ___ % OFT-V ____
S OFT-P ___ % OFT-P ____

***Peer Comparison**

S AET ___ % AET ____
S PET ___ % PET ____
S OFT-M ___ % OFT-M ____
S OFT-V ___ % OFT-V ____
S OFT-P ___ % OFT-P ____

Teacher

S TDI ___
% TDI ___
Total Intervals Observed ______

STEP 2

♦♦♦

Assessing Curriculum Placement

♦

Reading

In a direct assessment of reading, the oral reading rate is typically the metric used to assess student progress. However, this metric is only one of several that can be used for conducting a curriculum-based assessment of reading. When the examiner is interested in using a metric that may be more sensitive to changes in comprehension skills, two measures that may have value are a cloze technique and an oral retell technique. A cloze technique presents a student with a reading passage in which certain words have been eliminated; the student's task is to supply the missing words. Fuchs, Hamlett, and Fuchs (1990) have developed a computer program that provides a modified cloze technique in which the student is provided with a choice of three possible words, only one of which makes sense in the paragraph. Although only available for the Apple series computers, the program has been shown to be a potentially accurate method for monitoring progress in reading over time (Fuchs, Fuchs, Hamlett, & Allinder, 1991). Interested readers should consult both the Fuchs et al. (1991) article and the computer program for detailed descriptions of this modified cloze technique.

The use of oral retell techniques may also be a valuable adjunct to a curriculum-based assessment of reading. In this technique, students are asked to read a passage and then retell the story in their own words. The task can be done with both silent and oral reading if the evaluator suspects a student to be having difficulties when asked to read aloud. The student's responses can be scored using a checklist or rating scale such as that provided in Figure 7. This particular form is useful for narrative passages, but a similar type of checklist can be developed for more expository text.

ORAL RETELL TECHNIQUE

Step 1: The examiner selects a passage for the student to read. The passage should be between 250 and 300 words for a student in grade 3 or above, or between 150 and 200 words for a student in grades 1–2. The passage used should also have a story or theme embedded in it.

Step 2: The examiner asks the student to read the entire passage aloud, and times the reading (first minute only) to determine the rates of words read correctly and of errors per minute.

Step 3: The examiner then asks the student to retell the story in his/her own words, and tape-records the response for later scoring. The retell should be done in the following sequence. If the student is able to complete the retell accurately according to Level A procedures, then Levels B, C, and D need not be done. The examiner should proceed to the next level of the retell technique if the student is unsuccessful at the preceding level.

Level A: *Nonprompted retell without passage.* The examiner asks the student to retell without allowing him/her access to the passage. When the student cannot add anything else to the retell, he/she is stopped.

Level B: *Nonprompted retell with passage.* The examiner asks the student to retell, allowing him/her access to the passage. Again, when the student cannot add anything else to the retell, he/she is stopped.

Level C: *Prompted retell without passage.* The examiner does not allow the student access to the passage, but provides the student with a simple prompt about the story. For example, for the story described in the case example below, the examiner might ask the student, "The main idea of this story was about a circus coming to town. Now tell me more about the story." The examiner can continue to prompt the student, to see how many prompts are needed in order for the student to accurately recall the information read. The student is stopped when he/she cannot recall anything further.

Level D: *Prompted retell with access to passage.* The student is allowed to look at the passage as the examiner provides a simple prompt about the story. For example, for this story the examiner might ask the student, "The main idea of this story was about a circus coming to town. Now tell me more about the story." Again, the examiner can continue to prompt the student, to see how many prompts are needed in order for the student to accurately recall the information read. The student is stopped when he/she cannot recall anything further.

Step 4: The examiner scores the retell against the retelling scoring form provided or developed for the passage. Again, an example of such a scoring form is provided below.

A variation of the retell technique would ask the student to read the story silently to himself/herself rather than aloud.

QUANTIFICATION OF RETELLING FOR NARRATIVE TEXT

Student's name ________________________________

Book/Page: ________________________________ **Date:** ______________

Directions: Place a 1 next to each item the student includes in his/her retelling. Credit the gist as well as the obvious recall. Place an "*" if you ask the child questions to aid his/her recall.

	Level A	B	C	D	
Story Sense					
Theme: Main idea or moral of story	☐	☐	☐	☐	(1)
Problem: Difficulty to overcome	☐	☐	☐	☐	(1)
Goal: What the character wants to happen	☐	☐	☐	☐	(1)
Title: Name of the story (if possible)	☐	☐	☐	☐	(1)
Setting					
When and where the story occurs	☐	☐	☐	☐	(1)
Characters					
Name the main characters	☐	☐	☐	☐	(1)
Events/Episodes					
Initiating event	☐	☐	☐	☐	(1)
Major events (climax)	☐	☐	☐	☐	(1)
Sequence: Retells in structural order	☐	☐	☐	☐	(1)
Resolution					
Name problem solution for the goal	☐	☐	☐	☐	(.5)
End the story	☐	☐	☐	☐	(.5)
TOTAL	__	__	__	__	

FIGURE 7. Quantification of Retelling Form.

RETELL TECHNIQUE: EXAMPLES AND EXERCISES

Case Descriptions

Shawn was a fourth-grade student in a general education classroom. He was selected by his teacher as an average-performing student in her classroom. Troy was a fourth-grade student in the same general education classroom as Shawn. His teacher selected him as a student having significant problems in reading in her class. Both students were asked to read the following passage and then to retell the story in their own words without use of the passage (Level A retell). After reading each student's retell, readers are invited to complete the Quantification of Retelling Form provided for each one. A completed form is provided on the following page in each case.

Passage Read

The people of Lone Tree, Texas, often wonder why the circus never comes to their town. Almost nobody remembers the one time, years ago, that the circus did come to town.

Lone Tree was a busy cowtown. Two trains stopped there each day. On Saturday night folks from miles around came to town—ranchers, cowboys, Indians, and homesteaders. Bearpaw Smith's store had just about everything that the people needed. But there was one thing missing. None of these people had ever seen the circus.

Then one day a silent stranger came to Lone Tree and plastered the walls of Bearpaw Smith's store with circus posters. The circus was coming to town! The people were so excited, they could hardly wait for the day of the show. The big day finally arrived, and it would be a day to remember.

An hour before showtime, the crowds on the midway and around the ticket wagon were already so great that it seemed impossible that the circus tent would be able to hold them all. And still the people came.

One of the latecomers was Clyde Jones, the mountain-lion hunter, with his pack of "lion hounds." The circus people said it was against the rules to take dogs into the tent. Clyde said his were the best hounds in the state, and where he went they went. The ticket taker answered that this was one place they were not going to go. If Clyde wanted to see the circus, he'd have to leave his dogs outside. Clyde grumbled, but he did want to see the circus, so he tied the hounds to tent stakes and left them howling after him as he went inside.

Example and exercise for retell results for Shawn are to be found on pages 56–58, and for Troy on pages 60–62.

Retell Results for Shawn

Rates: Words correct/minute = 131
Errors/minute = 0

Verbatim transcript: It's about a town in Texas, and they've never seen, like, a circus before, and they want to see it. And they know a store that has everything except for a circus. And one day the store gets plastered, and they find out there is going to be a circus coming, and when they see it they can't believe that everyone can all fit into the tent. And then there is a man that comes late and he has, like, hounds and he can't bring them in, so he just leaves them out. But he wanted to bring them in, but he had to leave them outside.

Instructions: On the next page, score Shawn's retelling for Level A before looking at the scored form on page 58.

Exercise 1: Blank Form for Shawn

QUANTIFICATION OF RETELLING FOR NARRATIVE TEXT

Student's name ______________________

Book/Page: ______________________ **Date:** ____________

Directions: Place a 1 next to each item the student includes in his/her retelling. Credit the gist as well as the obvious recall. Place an "*" if you ask the child questions to aid his/her recall.

	Level A	Level B	Level C	Level D	
Story Sense					
Theme: Main idea or moral of story	☐	☐	☐	☐	(1)
Problem: Difficulty to overcome	☐	☐	☐	☐	(1)
Goal: What the character wants to happen	☐	☐	☐	☐	(1)
Title: Name of the story (if possible)	☐	☐	☐	☐	(1)
Setting					
When and where the story occurs	☐	☐	☐	☐	(1)
Characters					
Name the main characters	☐	☐	☐	☐	(1)
Events/Episodes					
Initiating event	☐	☐	☐	☐	(1)
Major events (climax)	☐	☐	☐	☐	(1)
Sequence: Retells in structural order	☐	☐	☐	☐	(1)
Resolution					
Name problem solution for the goal	☐	☐	☐	☐	(.5)
End the story	☐	☐	☐	☐	(.5)
TOTAL	_	_	_	_	

Exercise 1: Scored Form for Shawn

QUANTIFICATION OF RETELLING FOR NARRATIVE TEXT

Student's name Shawn

Book/Page: ________________ **Date:** ________

Directions: Place a 1 next to each item the student includes in his/her retelling. Credit the gist as well as the obvious recall. Place an "*" if you ask the child questions to aid his/her recall.

	Level A	Level B	Level C	Level D	
Story Sense					
Theme: Main idea or moral of story	☒	☐	☐	☐	(1)
Problem: Difficulty to overcome	☒	☐	☐	☐	(1)
Goal: What the character wants to happen	☒	☐	☐	☐	(1)
Title: Name of the story (if possible)	☐	☐	☐	☐	(1)
Setting					
When and where the story occurs	☒	☐	☐	☐	(1)
Characters					
Name the main characters	☐	☐	☐	☐	(1)
Events/Episodes					
Initiating event	☒	☐	☐	☐	(1)
Major events (climax)	☒	☐	☐	☐	(1)
Sequence: Retells in structural order	☒	☐	☐	☐	(1)
Resolution					
Name problem solution for the goal	☒	☐	☐	☐	(.5)
End the story	☒	☐	☐	☐	(.5)
TOTAL	8	__	__	__	

Comment

Note that Shawn's performance at Level A suggests no need to move to other levels of the retell technique.

Retell Results for Troy

Rates:	Words correct/minute = 55 Errors/minute = 3
Verbatim transcript:	(*Long pause*). The people are saying there has never been a circus in town before. So one day they heard there was a circus coming to town. Everybody was so happy they couldn't wait for the day to come. (*Examiner: Anything else?*) No.
Instructions:	On the next page, score Troy's retelling for Level A before looking at the scored form on page 62.

Exercise 2: Blank Form for Troy

QUANTIFICATION OF RETELLING FOR NARRATIVE TEXT

Student's name ____________________

Book/Page: ____________________ **Date:** ____________

Directions: Place a 1 next to each item the student includes in his/her retelling. Credit the gist as well as the obvious recall. Place an "*" if you ask the child questions to aid his/her recall.

	Level A	Level B	Level C	Level D	
Story Sense					
Theme: Main idea or moral of story	☐	☐	☐	☐	(1)
Problem: Difficulty to overcome	☐	☐	☐	☐	(1)
Goal: What the character wants to happen	☐	☐	☐	☐	(1)
Title: Name of the story (if possible)	☐	☐	☐	☐	(1)
Setting					
When and where the story occurs	☐	☐	☐	☐	(1)
Characters					
Name the main characters	☐	☐	☐	☐	(1)
Events/Episodes					
Initiating event	☐	☐	☐	☐	(1)
Major events (climax)	☐	☐	☐	☐	(1)
Sequence: Retells in structural order	☐	☐	☐	☐	(1)
Resolution					
Name problem solution for the goal	☐	☐	☐	☐	(.5)
End the story	☐	☐	☐	☐	(.5)
TOTAL	__	__	__	__	

Exercise 2: Scored Form for Troy

QUANTIFICATION OF RETELLING FOR NARRATIVE TEXT

Student's name Troy

Book/Page: ______ **Date:** ______

Directions: Place a 1 next to each item the student includes in his/her retelling. Credit the gist as well as the obvious recall. Place an "*" if you ask the child questions to aid his/her recall.

		Level A	B	C	D	
Story Sense						
Theme:	Main idea or moral of story	☒	☐	☐	☐	(1)
Problem:	Difficulty to overcome	☐	☐	☐	☐	(1)
Goal:	What the character wants to happen	☐	☐	☐	☐	(1)
Title:	Name of the story (if possible)	☐	☐	☐	☐	(1)
Setting						
When and where the story occurs		☐	☐	☐	☐	(1)
Characters						
Name the main characters		☐	☐	☐	☐	(1)
Events/Episodes						
Initiating event		☒	☐	☐	☐	(1)
Major events (climax)		☐	☐	☐	☐	(1)
Sequence: Retells in structural order		☐	☐	☐	☐	(1)
Resolution						
Name problem solution for the goal		☐	☐	☐	☐	(.5)
End the story		☐	☐	☐	☐	(.5)
	TOTAL	2	—	—	—	

Comment

Given the poor performance of Troy, the examiner would continue through the levels of prompted retell.

♦♦♦

Math

♦

One of the key aspects of curriculum-based assessment of math is using "digits correct per minute" as a metric in the scoring of student performance. In addition, in order to develop more effective interventions, examiners need to be able to conduct an analysis of the types of errors students are making as they complete the math probes. This section of the workbook provides descriptions of how to score math probes using digits correct per minute, along with examples of conducting an analysis of errors. Practice exercises for both scoring and interpretation of math probes are included.

USING DIGITS CORRECT PER MINUTE IN SCORING MATH PROBES: RATIONALE

Typically, when a student is asked to complete math problems, the teacher marks the student's responses as either correct or incorrect. Even small and minor errors in the computation process can result in the student's obtaining an incorrect answer. In assessing the outcomes of an instructional process, an examiner needs to use a metric that can be sensitive to the student's gradual acquisition across time of the skills required to complete computations accurately. The metric of digits correct rather than problems correct accomplishes this goal.

For example, a student asked to add two 3-digit numbers may initially get 0 digits correct:

(1)

$$\begin{array}{r} 356 \\ +\,678 \\ \hline 922 \end{array}$$

Recognizing the student's lack of knowledge of regrouping principles, the teacher begins to teach the student how to regroup from the 1's to the 10's column. After some instruction, the student now does the following when given a similar type of problem:

(2)

$$\begin{array}{r} 467 \\ +\ 589 \\ \hline 946 \end{array}$$

This problem shows the student to have 1 digit correct. After additional instruction, the student produces the results of problem 3:

(3)

$$\begin{array}{r} 378 \\ +\ 657 \\ \hline 1035 \end{array}$$

The metric of digits correct makes the student's gradual acquisition of the regrouping concept evident. If the evaluator were to use only the problem's correctness or incorrectness to determine whether the student was learning the concept of regrouping, the student's gradual acquisition of the skill would not be evident.

SCORING DIGITS CORRECT FOR ADDITION AND SUBTRACTION PROBLEMS

The calculation of digits correct when the student is completing addition or subtraction problems is fairly straightforward. Each correct digit *below* the answer line is counted. If the problem involves regrouping, and the student places numbers above the columns to indicate how much was carried to the next column, these numbers are not counted in the digits-correct figure.

Examples:

$$\begin{array}{r} 12 \\ +4 \\ \hline 16 \end{array} \text{ (2 digits correct)} \qquad \begin{array}{r} 145 \\ +\ 672 \\ \hline 817 \end{array} \text{ (3 digits correct)}$$

$$\begin{array}{r} 54 \\ -\ 27 \\ \hline 27 \end{array} \text{ (2 digits correct)} \qquad \begin{array}{r} 2675 \\ -\ 1089 \\ \hline 1586 \end{array} \text{ (4 digits correct)}$$

In a math curriculum-based assessment, sets of problems are adminstered under timed conditions, and a calculation is made of the number of digits correct per minute. Exercise 3 provides an opportunity to practice scoring addition and subtraction math problems using digits correct per minute.

Exercise 3: Digits Correct for Addition and Subtraction Problems

Addition and subtraction facts with regrouping to 10's column.

A 15 - 9 = 6	B 4 - 0 = 4	C 76 + 17 = 81	D 12 - 8 = 4	E 1 + 8 = 9
F 8 + 3 = 11	G 76 + 6 = 82	H 80 - 4 = 84	I 47 - 38 = 11	J 10 - 5 = 5
K 2 + 8 = 10	L 0 + 6 = 6	M 57 - 9 = 52	N 431 - 31 = 400	O 15 + 66 = 81

Scoring: Write in the number of digits correct and incorrect for each problem.

Problem	Digits Correct	Digits Incorrect
A		
B		
C		
D		
E		
F		
G		
H		
I		
J		
K		
L		
M		
N		
O		
TOTAL		

Answer Key to Exercise 3

Problem	Digits Correct	Digits Incorrect
A	1	0
B	1	0
C	0	2
D	1	0
E	1	0
F	2	0
G	2	0
H	0	2
I	0	2
J	1	0
K	2	0
L	1	0
M	0	2
N	3	0
O	2	0
TOTAL	17	8

Comments

The results of this math probe show several things. First, the digits-correct data place the student within the instructional level (10–19 digits correct) for students working within second-grade materials. However, the digits-incorrect results show that the student is making too many errors to be considered instructional (3–7 errors would be instructional). Therefore, the outcome of the probe would demonstrate that the student is in the frustrational level for second-grade material. A careful examination of the probe, however, shows specifically the type of skills that the student has yet to learn. The results show that the student knows basic addition and subtraction facts. However, whenever faced with a problem where regrouping was required, the student instead subtracted the lower from the higher number. The probe suggests that the student has not yet acquired the knowledge of how to regroup in subtraction. Interestingly, the results of problems G and O indicate that the difficulties in regrouping may be specific to subtraction.

Make Up Your Own Problem Exercise Here

A	B	C	D	E
F	G	H	I	J
K	L	M	N	O

Scoring

Problem	Digits Correct	Digits Incorrect
A		
B		
C		
D		
E		
F		
G		
H		
I		
J		
K		
L		
M		
N		
O		
TOTAL		

SCORING DIGITS CORRECT FOR MULTIPLICATION PROBLEMS

When multiplication is the skill assessed, counting digits correct can become more complicated. If the problem involves double-digit multiplication, then several digits are usually written below the answer line prior to reaching the final response. Because double-digit multiplication involves the operations of both multiplication and addition, a student could potentially make errors in two types of problems. That is, a student could multiply correctly but add incorrectly, thus getting the wrong answer. Likewise, a student could multiply incorrectly but add correctly, again reaching the wrong answer. If the student were to be given credit only for both multiplying *and* adding correctly, a student could be penalized unduly for performing only one incorrect operation. Given that metrics need to be sensitive to change over time, this would be inappropriate.

As a general rule of thumb, when digits correct are used in scoring multiplication, a student is given credit for the digit if the operation was performed correctly even if the answer itself is incorrect. For example, if a student asked to multiply 2 digits by 2 digits did the following:

75
× 26
450
150_
28**50**

the problem would be scored by counting all digits correct below the answer line. This problem has a total of 9 digits correct (indicated in bold) and 2 incorrect. Seven of the correct digits are the numbers 450 and 150(0), the last 0 being a place holder, and 2 digits are correct in the final answer. Thus, this student multiplied correctly but added incorrectly. The score suggests that the difficulties were in the addition portion of the problem, since the majority of digits would be scored for multiplication rather than addition.

In contrast, another student performing the same problem may have done the following:

75
× 26
435
285**_**
341**5**

This problem would be scored as having 4 digits correct (shown in bold): 1 digit (the 0 place holder) under the 1's column under the answer line, plus the 3 digits showing correct multiplication and addition. In this case, the student multiplied mostly incorrectly and added only partially correctly. Again, counting all digits except the placeholder incorrect would penalize the student unduly, when the real difficulty is only in multiplication—not in addition or in understanding the correct method for setting up a double-digit multiplication problem.

Exercise 4 is provided for the reader to practice scoring 2- and 3-digit multiplication problems.

Exercise 4: Digits Correct for Two- and Three-Digit Multiplication Problems

A 11 × 13 13 11_ 123	B 83 × 48 644 127_ 1914	C 27 × 34 108 81_ 918	D 756 × 8 5648	E 113 × 59 1017 668_ 7697
F 550 × 66 3300 1216_ 15460	G 186 × 59 1676 4530 6106	H 536 × 91 536 4824_ 48776	I 710 × 92 1420 6390_ 65320	J 284 × 67 1988 1704_ 19028

Scoring: Write in the number of digits correct and incorrect for each problem.

Problem	Digits Correct	Digits Incorrect
A		
B		
C		
D		
E		
F		
G		
H		
I		
J		
TOTAL		

Answer Key to Exercise 4

Problem	Digits Correct	Digits Incorrect
A	7	1
B	7	4
C	9	0
D	2	2
E	10	2
F	10	4
G	7	5
H	13	0
I	14	0
J	14	0

Comments

The results of this probe show that the student, in general, understands the procedure for conducting 2- and 3-digit multiplication. Errors in place value or setup of the problems are not evident. However, the student does make the mistake of operations when the second digit is supposed to be multiplied. On problems B and F, for example the student added instead of multiplied. On problem G, the student erred in place values, which resulted in many errors. Finally, it is important to remember to give the student credit for leaving a blank (0 place holder) in the appropriate columns in most problems. It should also be noted that when the student multiplied incorrectly, he/she sometimes added correctly. Thus, credit is given for the student's completing the operation correctly.

Make Up Your Own Problem Exercise Here

A	B	C	D	E
F	G	H	I	J
K	L	M	N	O

Problem	Digits Correct	Digits Incorrect
A		
B		
C		
D		
E		
F		
G		
H		
I		
J		
K		
L		
M		
N		
O		
TOTAL		

SCORING DIGITS CORRECT FOR DIVISION PROBLEMS

Division problems create several unique problems in the scoring of digits correct. Division involving two or more digits requires that students perform three operations–division, multiplication, and subtraction. However, because of the complexity in division, the rule of thumb that is applied is to count the digit incorrect only if the incorrect operation is performed, or if incorrect place values are used. For example, in the following example, the student begins the division problem correctly. (The student's work is shown on the left; the problem done entirely correctly is shown on the right.)

283	295
25)7375	25)7375
50	50
237	237
200	225
75	125
50	125
25	0

The student multiplies correctly. He/she makes an error in division, and then errs in subtraction. The multiplication is correct, as is the final subtraction. The student is unsure of what to do with the remainder, which is of course incorrect in the problem. In this problem, the student scores 7 digits correct (see the items in bold) out of the total 18 possible digits. Although counting the number of digits correct per minute is a common metric, another approach to scoring division is to count the percentage of digits correct out of the total possible. In this example, the student would have had 7/18, or 38.9% digits correct. Exercise 5 provides opportunities to practice scoring division problems for digits correct.

Exercise 5: Digits Correct for Division Problems

A 50 R3 14)703 70 3	B 1410 R2 3)452 3 15 12 32 30 2	C 10 R4 88)884 88 04 0 4	D 941 11)995 99 050 44 11	E 303 29)8787 87 8 0 87 87 0

Scoring: Write in the number of actual and possible digits correct for each problem.

Problem	Possible Correct	Actual Correct
A		
B		
C		
D		
E		

Answer Key to Exercise 5

Problem	Possible Correct	Actual Correct
A	6	6
B	10	4
C	6	6
D	6	2
E	9	9

Comments

Notice that when a remainder is present, the student is given an additional digit credit for indicating a correct remainder next to the answer. The student is not given additional credit for remainders of 0, nor is he/she given credit for the addition of unnecessary digits (such as a 0 in problem C).

Make Up Your Own Problem Exercise Here

A	B	C	D	E
F	G	H	I	J
K	L	M	N	O

Problem	Possible Correct	Actual Incorrect
A		
B		
C		
D		
E		
F		
G		
H		
I		
J		
K		
L		
M		
N		
O		
TOTAL		

Spelling

USING CORRECT LETTER SEQUENCES IN SCORING SPELLING: RATIONALE

As we have just seen, an examiner provides students with partial credit for responses in math by using digits correct as a metric, rather than simply problems correct. An analogous metric exists for spelling—"correct letter sequences." By counting the number of correct consecutive letters, rather than just the words spelled completely correctly, the examiner can detect small improvements in a student's responses. In addition, the types of errors made can be diagnostic; they can help the examiner identify the skills that a student has mastered and the ones that need to be targeted in future interventions.

Scoring correct letter sequences can be quite tedious and time-consuming. Fuchs, Fuchs, and Hamlett (1990) have devised a computer program that will provide the evaluator with automatic scoring for correct letter sequences. Although the program will only work with the word lists provided by Fuchs et al. (1990), the program's output offers extensive diagnostic information for the teacher in designing instructional programs (see Figures 8 and 9). Unfortunately, the computer program is only available for the Apple series computers, and upgrades to more sophisticated hardware are not anticipated.

NAME: Charles Landrum	Spelling 4	Date: 4/10	Page 1

Corrects (100% LS)	14 word(s)
Near Misses (60–99% LS)	19 word(s)
Moderate Misses (20–59% LS)	16 word(s)
Far Misses (0–19% LS)	1 word(s)

Type	Correct	Possible	Pct	Type	Correct	Possible	Pct
Sing cons	48	50	96	Final vow	3	7	42
Blend	7	10	70	Double	3	4	75
FSLZ	0	0	100	c/s	0	1	0
Single vow	21	31	67	c/ck	0	2	0
Digraph	6	8	75	-le	4	7	57
Vowel + N	6	8	75	ch/tch	2	2	100
Dual cons	13	25	52	-dge	0	1	0
Final e	1	5	20	Vowel team	4	12	33
igh/ign	0	0	100	Suffix	5	6	83
ild/old	0	0	100	tion/sion	0	1	0
a + l + cons	0	0	100	ance/ence	0	0	100
Vowel + R	9	14	64	sure/ture	0	0	100

KEY ERRORS

Dual cons	Final e	Final vow
learner–leaner	alone–alon	taste–tast
sample–samble	knife–knif	hero–hearow
chart–chard	rare–rar	lazy–lazz
mumble–mobble	cube–cub	unlucky–unluke
tactor–trater		
apart–apeot		

FIGURE 8. Example of page 1 of a curriculum-based measurement (CBM) skills analysis in spelling. From "Effects of expert system advice within curriculum-based measurement on teacher planning and student achievement in spelling," by L. S. Fuchs, D. Fuchs, C. L. Hamlett, & R. M. Allinder, 1991, *School Psychology Review, 20*, p. 56. Copyright 1991 by the National Association of School Psychologists. Reprinted by permission.

NAME: Charles Landrum		Spelling 0	Date: 9/1	Page 2
Corrects (100% LS)				
100	March . . . . March			
100	death . . . . death			
100	sometimes . . . . somtimes			
100	thankful. . . . . . . thankful			
100	baker. . . . . baker			
100	uncover . . . . . . uncover			
100	shy . . . . shy			
100	weakness . . . . . weakness			
100	forgot . . . . forgot			
100	eyes . . . . eyes			
100	army . . . . army			
100	powerless . . . . . powerless			
100	wife. . . . . wife			
100	mix . . . . mix			
Near Misses (60%–99% LS)				
77	shipment. . . . . . shapment	Single vow		
75	instead . . . . insted	Vowel team		
75	patches. . . . . . . patces	Digraph		
75	moisten. . . . . . . mosten	Vowel team		
75	quieter . . . . quiter	Vowel team		
75	learner . . . . leaner	Dual cons		
75	trouble . . . . trubble	Vowel temam		
71	sample . . . . samble	Dual cons		
71	listen. . . . . lesten	Single vow		
66	badge . . . . bage	-dge		
66	taste . . . . tast	Final vow		
66	chart . . . . chard	Dual cons		
66	alone. . . . . alon	Final e		
66	restless . . . . reasless	Blend		
66	knife . . . . knif	Final e		
60	hero . . . . hearow	Final vow	Vowel + R	
60	rare . . . . rar	Final e		
60	cube . . . . cub	Final e		
60	lazy . . . . lazz	Final vow		
Moderate Misses (20–59% LS)				
57	tickle. . . . . teakle	c/ck	Single vow	
57	French. . . . . fanch	Vowel + N	Blend	
57	mumble . . . . . . mobble	Dual cons	Single vow	
50	unlucky. . . . . . . unluke	Final vow	c/ck	
50	tractor. . . . . tater	Vowel + R	Dual cons	
50	apart . . . . apeot	Vowel + R	Dual cons	
44	calendar . . . . . . cander	Vowel + R	Vowel + N	Sing cons
42	mumble . . . . . . mommbe	-le	Single vow	
40	rail. . . . . real	Vowel team		
37	station. . . . . stanch	tion/sion		
28	sample . . . . scembe	-le	Dual cons	Single vow
25	certain . . . . chanten	Vowel team	Vowel + R	c/s
25	squeeze . . . . . . scease	Vowel team	Digraph	Sing cons
20	limb. . . . . lem	Dual cons	Single vow	
20	treatment . . . . . tempemt	Suffix	Vowel team	Blend
20	limb. . . . . leam	Dual cons	Single vow	
Far Misses (0–19% LS)				
14	giggle . . . . gelly	-le	Double	Single vow

FIGURE 9. Example of page 2 of a CBM skills analysis in spelling. From "Effects of expert system advice within curriculum-based measurement on teacher planning and student achievement in spelling," by L. S. Fuchs, D. Fuchs, C. L. Hamlett, & R. M. Allinder, 1991, *School Psychology Review, 20*, p. 57. Copyright 1991 by the National Association of School Psychologists. Reprinted with permission.

SCORING CORRECT LETTER SEQUENCES

Step 1: The examiner places a blank before the first and last letter of each word to be scored. The blank is considered as a correct phantom character and is used to enable the initial and ending letters of words to be counted. For example:

_ s a m p l e _

Step 2: A linking symbol (⌒) is used to connect each letter to the next, beginning with the initial blank before the first letter. These should be placed alternately above and below consecutive letters:

_⌒s‿a⌒m‿p⌒l‿e⌒_

Step 3: The examiner counts the number of letter sequences that are correct. The word "sample" above has a total of 7 possible correct letter sequences.

Special Scoring Situations: Certain words create a need for special rules and conventions. In particular, the presence of double consonants can be confusing when the letter sequences metric is being used. If the student omits one of the consonants, credit is only given once. Comparing the student's spelling with the correct spelling can make this evident. For example, the word

_⌒b‿u⌒b‿b⌒l‿e⌒_

contains a total of 7 possible letter sequences. A student who spells the word

_⌒b‿u⌒b‿l⌒e‿_

would be scored as having 5 letter sequences correct. The connections between "_" and "b," "b" and "u," and "u" and "b" are correct. The lack of the second "b" results in an incorrect sequence between the two "b's" and the "b" and "l" (no second "b"), but other sequences are correct.

Sample exercises for practicing scoring of spelling using correct letter sequences are provided below.

Exercise 6: Scoring Correct Letter Sequences for Spelling

Instructions: Listed below are the actual ways in which a student spelled words on a weekly spelling test. The correct spellings are provided in the next column. Indicate the number of correct letter sequences for each word. The following page provides an answer sheet.

Word Spelled by Student	Correct Spelling	Letter Sequences Correct/Total Possible	Word Spelled Correctly?
rain	rain		
belong	belong		
botin	button		
slat	salt		
clock	clock		
smart	smart		
stap	step		
shep	sheep		
mint	minute		
above	above		
greup	group		
hunt	hut		
kesz	crazy		
jock	joke		
mire	mirror		
riad	drove		
nose	noise		

Answer Sheet for Exercise 6

Note: The first two words are scored as examples.

Word Spelled by Student	Correct Spelling	Letter Sequences Correct/Total Possible	Word Spelled Correctly?
_ r a i n _	rain	5/5	✓
_ b e l o n g _	belong	7/7	✓
botin	button	2/7	
slat	salt	2/5	
clock	clock	6/6	✓
smart	smart	6/6	✓
stap	step	3/5	
shep	sheep	4/6	
mint	minute	3/7	
above	above	6/6	✓
greup	group	4/6	
hunt	hut	3/4	
kesz	crazy	0/6	
jock	joke	2/5	
mire	mirror	3/7	
riad	drove	0/6	
nose	noise	4/6	

Exercise 7: Scoring Correct Letter Sequences for Spelling

Instructions: Listed below are the actual ways in which a student spelled words on a weekly spelling test. The correct spellings are provided in the next column. Indicate the number of correct letter sequences for each word. The following page provides an answer sheet.

Word Spelled by Student	Correct Spelling	Letter Sequences Correct/Total Possible	Word Spelled Correctly?
scad	scold		
srer	sorry		
tow	tall		
hapin	happen		
fi	fourth		
alive	alive		
give	given		
dip	drop		
terth	teeth		
beer	bear		
beck	drink		
sotp	stop		
north	north		
jell	jail		
thre	flower		
leve	leave		
insiad	inside		

Answer Sheet for Exercise 7

Note: The first two words are scored as examples.

Word Spelled by Student	Correct Spelling	Letter Sequences Correct/Total Possible	Word Spelled Correctly?
_ s c a d _	scold	3/6	
_ s r e y _	sorry	2/6	
tow	tall	1/5	
hapin	happen	4/7	
fi	fourth	1/7	
alive	alive	6/6	✓
give	given	4/6	
dip	drop	2/5	
terth	teeth	4/6	
beer	bear	3/5	
beck	drink	1/6	
sotp	stop	2/5	
north	north	6/6	✓
jell	jail	2/5	
thre	flower	0/7	
leve	leave	4/6	
insiad	inside	4/7	

♦♦♦

Written Language

♦

Written language assessments collected as part of the assessment of academic skills problems can be scored in multiple ways. Each of these metrics is used for a somewhat different purpose.

SCORING FOR WORDS WRITTEN

The simplest metric is to count the total number of words written. This metric is a strategy commonly used when the purpose of the assessment is progress monitoring. When an evaluator is using this metric, a word is counted if it is separated from other words in the written material. Words are counted regardless of whether they are spelled correctly or are phonetically recognizable. For example, a student given the story starter "When my video game started predicting the future, I knew I had to . . ." wrote the following during a 3-minute period:

> "got my mom to check it out I was ckerd it was hard to recat but my mom holped me then my brather came in to my room he holped me to but he left my room want down."

Notice that many of the words are not recognizable, nor did they make sense in the context of the story as subsequently dictated by the student. The number of words written, however, would be scored as 39.

SCORING FOR WRITING MECHANICS

When the evaluator is interested more in short-term monitoring and the development of effective interventions, strengths and weaknesses in the mechanics of writing need to be assessed. This is most easily accomplished by developing a checklist that can be used repeatedly after each written language assessment is administered. Figure 10 provides an example of a quality evaluation measure that one can use for assessing mechanics such as capitalization, punctuation, sentence construction, paragraph construction, and appearance of the written product.

ASSESSING QUALITY OF LONGER WRITING SAMPLES

The evaluator may also be interested in the overall quality of the student's writing. Overall quality can be assessed by using holistic scoring metrics for longer, more elaborate assignments given as part of the instructional process. These measures usually assign scores on a scale (such as 1 to 5), with the criteria for each score described. Examples of two types of these scoring devices are provided in Figures 11 and 12.

QUALITY EVALUATION MEASURE FOR WRITTEN PRODUCTS

Elementary Level

Student Name: ____________________
Date: ____________________
Grade: ________

Rating Scale:

3 = Skill used consistently throughout written product (>95% of time)

2 = Skill used frequently throughout written product (>50% of time)

1 = Skill used infrequently or inaccurately (<50% of time)

0 = No evidence of skill

Capitalization					
First words in sentences are capitalized		0	1	2	3
Proper nouns are capitalized		0	1	2	3
Capitals are not used improperly		0	1	2	3
Punctuation					
Punctuation occurs at the end of each sentence		0	1	2	3
End punctuation is correct		0	1	2	3
Sentence Construction					
Absence of run-on sentences		0	1	2	3
Absence of sentence fragments		0	1	2	3
Absence of nonsensical sentences		0	1	2	3
Paragraph Construction					
Each paragraph contains a topic sentence	N/A	0	1	2	3
Each sentence within a paragraph relates to the topic sentence	N/A	0	1	2	3
Appearance of Written Product					
Words are legible		0	1	2	3
Spacing is appropriate between letters/words		0	1	2	3
Margins are appropriate		0	1	2	3
Written product is neat with correct spelling		0	1	2	3

TOTAL SCORE ______

FIGURE 10. Measure for assessing written language skills during 3-minute story starters.

Criteria for Holistic Writing Assessment

1. Highly flawed—Not competent Ideas poorly communicated Frequent usage errors (such as agreement, pronoun misuse, tense) Incorrect or erratic use of capitalization, punctuation, and spelling conventions Sentence fragments and run-ons; few complete sentences No concept of paragraph construction	2. Unacceptable—Not competent Poor organization of ideas Frequent usage errors (such as agreement, pronoun misuse, tense) Inconsistent use of capitalization, punctuation, and spelling conventions Sentence fragments and run-ons; few complete sentences Poor topic sentence; flawed paragraph development
3. Minimally competent—Acceptable Ideas sufficiently organized and communicated Only occasional usage errors (such as agreement, pronoun misuse, tense) Minimal number of sentence errors (fragments or run-ons) Paragraphs have topic sentences, supporting ideas, and closing sentences Some attempt at paragraph transition	4. Competent—Clear mastery Ideas clearly communicated and of a fairly mature quality No usage errors Correct capitalization, punctuation, and spelling No fragments or run-ons Effective paragraph construction

Note: A paper that is illegible, off the point, or a nonresponse is scored 0.

FIGURE 11. Measure for assessing written language skills during longer written assignments. Source: Division of Curriculum and Instruction, Department of Elementary and Secondary Education, Milwaukee Public Schools, Milwaukee, Wisconsin.

Criteria for Analytical Scoring

	1	2	3	4	5	
Organization	Little or nothing is written. The essay is disorganized, incoherent, and poorly developed. The essay does not stay on the topic.		The essay is not complete. It lacks an introduction, well-developed body, or conclusion. The coherence and sequence are attempted, but not adequate.		The essay is well-organized. It contains an introductory supporting and concluding paragraph. The essay is coherent, ordered logically, and fully developed.	x6
Sentence Structure	The student writes frequent run-ons or fragments.		The student makes occasional errors in sentence structure. Little variety in sentence length or structure exists.		The sentences are complete and varied in length and structure.	x5
Usage	The student makes frequent errors in word choice and agreement.		The student makes occasional errors in word choice or agreement.		The usage is correct. Word choice is appropriate.	x4
Mechanics	The student makes frequent errors in spelling, punctuation, and capitalization.		The student makes an occasional error in mechanics.		The spelling, capitalization, and punctuation are correct.	x4
Format	The format is sloppy. There are no margins or indentations. Handwriting is inconsistent.		The handwriting, margins, and indentations have occasional inconsistencies—no titles or inappropriate title.		The format is correct. The title is appropriate. The handwriting, margins, and indentations are consistent.	x1

FIGURE 12. Measure for assessing written language skills during longer written assignments. Source: Adams County School District No. 12, Northglenn, Colorado.

SCORING BRIEF WRITTEN LANGUAGE SAMPLES: EXAMPLES AND EXERCISES

Below are three written samples, collected as 3-minute story starters during a direct assessment of written expression. All students were in the 5th grade. In the exercises below, readers can practice using the Quality Evaluation Measure for Written Products, Elementary Level, to score the samples. A scored form follows each blank form (answers are underlined).

Starter and Writing Samples

Starter: When my video game started predicting the future, I knew I had to . . .

Student 1: Bryan

got my mom to check it out I was ckerd it was hard to recat but my mom holped me then my brother came in to my room he helped my to but he left my room want down.

Student 2: Valesa

Get it to put back on my other game and when the future came on my board I was very surprised because it was talking to me and I did not now wat it was talking about and it just kep on talking to me and when it said I was going to live in mars I said y must I live on mars he said because you have to and I said how comes.

Student 3: Cary

run and get my camera. I ran into my room to find it, it was gone. I wanted to see what it would do if I turned it off. I put my hand on the power button, and I felt a stinging shock on my finger. I ran to get my mom. By the time she got there, it was too late.

Exercise 9: Blank Form for Bryan

QUALITY EVALUATION MEASURE FOR WRITTEN PRODUCTS

Elementary Level

Student Name: ____________________

Date: ____________________

Grade: ________

Rating Scale:

3 = Skill used consistently throughout written product (>95% of time)

2 = Skill used frequently throughout written product (>50% of time)

1 = Skill used infrequently or inaccurately (<50% of time)

0 = No evidence of skill

Capitalization					
First words in sentences are capitalized		0	1	2	3
Proper nouns are capitalized		0	1	2	3
Capitals are not used improperly		0	1	2	3
Punctuation					
Punctuation occurs at the end of each sentence		0	1	2	3
End punctuation is correct		0	1	2	3
Sentence Construction					
Absence of run-on sentences		0	1	2	3
Absence of sentence fragments		0	1	2	3
Absence of nonsensical sentences		0	1	2	3
Paragraph Construction					
Each paragraph contains a topic sentence	N/A	0	1	2	3
Each sentence within a paragraph relates to the topic sentence	N/A	0	1	2	3
Appearance of Written Product					
Words are legible		0	1	2	3
Spacing is appropriate between letters/words		0	1	2	3
Margins are appropriate		0	1	2	3
Written product is neat with correct spelling		0	1	2	3

TOTAL SCORE ______

Exercise 9: Scored Form for Bryan

QUALITY EVALUATION MEASURE FOR WRITTEN PRODUCTS

Elementary Level

Student Name: Bryan
Date: 4-21-93
Grade: 5

Rating Scale:

3 = Skill used consistently throughout written product (>95% of time)

2 = Skill used frequently throughout written product (>50% of time)

1 = Skill used infrequently or inaccurately (<50% of time)

0 = No evidence of skill

Capitalization					
First words in sentences are capitalized		0	1	2	3
Proper nouns are capitalized		0	1	2	3
Capitals are not used improperly		0	1	2	3
Punctuation					
Punctuation occurs at the end of each sentence		0	1	2	3
End punctuation is correct		0	1	2	3
Sentence Construction					
Absence of run-on sentences		0	1	2	3
Absence of sentence fragments		0	1	2	3
Absence of nonsensical sentences		0	1	2	3
Paragraph Construction					
Each paragraph contains a topic sentence	N/A	0	1	2	3
Each sentence within a paragraph relates to the topic sentence	N/A	0	1	2	3
Appearance of Written Product					
Words are legible	N/A	0	1	2	3
Spacing is appropriate between letters/words	N/A	0	1	2	3
Margins are appropriate	N/A	0	1	2	3
Written product is neat with correct spelling	N/A	0	1	2	3

TOTAL SCORE 4

Exercise 10: Blank Form for Valesa

QUALITY EVALUATION MEASURE FOR WRITTEN PRODUCTS

Elementary Level

Student Name: ____________________

Date: ____________________

Grade: ________

Rating Scale:

3 = Skill used consistently throughout written product (>95% of time)

2 = Skill used frequently throughout written product (>50% of time)

1 = Skill used infrequently or inaccurately (<50% of time)

0 = No evidence of skill

Capitalization					
First words in sentences are capitalized		0	1	2	3
Proper nouns are capitalized		0	1	2	3
Capitals are not used improperly		0	1	2	3
Punctuation					
Punctuation occurs at the end of each sentence		0	1	2	3
End punctuation is correct		0	1	2	3
Sentence Construction					
Absence of run-on sentences		0	1	2	3
Absence of sentence fragments		0	1	2	3
Absence of nonsensical sentences		0	1	2	3
Paragraph Construction					
Each paragraph contains a topic sentence	N/A	0	1	2	3
Each sentence within a paragraph relates to the topic sentence	N/A	0	1	2	3
Appearance of Written Product					
Words are legible		0	1	2	3
Spacing is appropriate between letters/words		0	1	2	3
Margins are appropriate		0	1	2	3
Written product is neat with correct spelling		0	1	2	3

TOTAL SCORE ______

Exercise 10: Scored Form for Valesa

QUALITY EVALUATION MEASURE FOR WRITTEN PRODUCTS

Elementary Level

Student Name: <u>Valesa</u>
Date: <u>4-21-93</u>
Grade: <u>5</u>

Rating Scale:

3 = Skill used consistently throughout written product (>95% of time)
2 = Skill used frequently throughout written product (>50% of time)
1 = Skill used infrequently or inaccurately (<50% of time)
0 = No evidence of skill

Capitalization					
First words in sentences are capitalized		0	<u>1</u>	2	3
Proper nouns are capitalized		0	1	<u>2</u>	3
Capitals are not used improperly		0	1	2	<u>3</u>
Punctuation					
Punctuation occurs at the end of each sentence		<u>0</u>	1	2	3
End punctuation is correct		<u>0</u>	1	2	3
Sentence Construction					
Absence of run-on sentences		0	1	2	<u>3</u>
Absence of sentence fragments		0	1	2	<u>3</u>
Absence of nonsensical sentences		0	1	2	<u>3</u>
Paragraph Construction					
Each paragraph contains a topic sentence	<u>N/A</u>	0	1	2	3
Each sentence within a paragraph relates to the topic sentence	<u>N/A</u>	0	1	2	3
Appearance of Written Product					
Words are legible	<u>N/A</u>	0	1	2	3
Spacing is appropriate between letters/words	<u>N/A</u>	0	1	2	3
Margins are appropriate	<u>N/A</u>	0	1	2	3
Written product is neat with correct spelling	<u>N/A</u>	0	1	2	3

TOTAL SCORE <u>15</u>

Exercise 11: Blank Form for Cary

QUALITY EVALUATION MEASURE FOR WRITTEN PRODUCTS

Elementary Level

Student Name: ____________________

Date: ____________________

Grade: ________

Rating Scale:

3 = Skill used consistently throughout written product (>95% of time)

2 = Skill used frequently throughout written product (>50% of time)

1 = Skill used infrequently or inaccurately (<50% of time)

0 = No evidence of skill

Capitalization					
First words in sentences are capitalized		0	1	2	3
Proper nouns are capitalized		0	1	2	3
Capitals are not used improperly		0	1	2	3
Punctuation					
Punctuation occurs at the end of each sentence		0	1	2	3
End punctuation is correct		0	1	2	3
Sentence Construction					
Absence of run-on sentences		0	1	2	3
Absence of sentence fragments		0	1	2	3
Absence of nonsensical sentences		0	1	2	3
Paragraph Construction					
Each paragraph contains a topic sentence	N/A	0	1	2	3
Each sentence within a paragraph relates to the topic sentence	N/A	0	1	2	3
Appearance of Written Product					
Words are legible		0	1	2	3
Spacing is appropriate between letters/words		0	1	2	3
Margins are appropriate		0	1	2	3
Written product is neat with correct spelling		0	1	2	3

TOTAL SCORE ______

Exercise 11: Scored Form for Cary

QUALITY EVALUATION MEASURE FOR WRITTEN PRODUCTS
Elementary Level

Student Name: Cary

Date: 4-21-93

Grade: 5

Rating Scale:

3 = Skill used consistently throughout written product (>95% of time)

2 = Skill used frequently throughout written product (>50% of time)

1 = Skill used infrequently or inaccurately (<50% of time)

0 = No evidence of skill

Capitalization					
First words in sentences are capitalized		0	1	2	<u>3</u>
Proper nouns are capitalized		0	1	2	<u>3</u>
Capitals are not used improperly		0	1	2	<u>3</u>
Punctuation					
Punctuation occurs at the end of each sentence		0	1	2	<u>3</u>
End punctuation is correct		0	1	2	<u>3</u>
Sentence Construction					
Absence of run-on sentences		0	1	2	<u>3</u>
Absence of sentence fragments		0	1	2	<u>3</u>
Absence of nonsensical sentences		0	1	2	<u>3</u>
Paragraph Construction					
Each paragraph contains a topic sentence	<u>N/A</u>	0	1	2	3
Each sentence within a paragraph relates to the topic sentence	<u>N/A</u>	0	1	2	3
Appearance of Written Product					
Words are legible	<u>N/A</u>	0	1	2	3
Spacing is appropriate between letters/words	<u>N/A</u>	0	1	2	3
Margins are appropriate	<u>N/A</u>	0	1	2	3
Written product is neat with correct spelling	<u>N/A</u>	0	1	2	3

TOTAL SCORE 24

Summary Form for Academic Assessment

Data obtained during Steps 1 and 2 represent the collection of extensive information about a student's present level of academic performance. The data also provide a means of examining the academic environment in which the student's problems are occurring. To facilitate the process of assembling these data, a form for summarizing these data is provided.

DATA SUMMARY FORM FOR ACADEMIC ASSESSMENT

Child's Name: ____________________ **Teacher:** ____________________

Grade: ____________________ **School:** ____________________

Date: _____ **School District:** ____________________

READING—SKILLS

Primary type of reading series used

- ☐ Basal reader
- ☐ Literature-based
- ☐ Trade books

Secondary type of reading materials used

- ☐ Basal reader
- ☐ Literature-based
- ☐ Trade books
- ☐ None

Title of curriculum series ____________________

Level/book—target student ____________________

Level/book—average student ____________________

Results of Passages Administered

Grade level/book	Location in book	WC/ min	Errors/ min	% Correct	Median scores for level WC	ER	%C	Learning Level(M, I, F)
	Beginning							
	Middle							
	End							
	Beginning							
	Middle							
	End							
	Beginning							
	Middle							
	End							
	Beginning							
	Middle							
	End							

READING—ENVIRONMENT

Instructional Procedures

Primary type of reading instruction

☐ Basal readers ☐ Whole language

☐ Other (describe) ______________________________

Number of reading groups ______________________________

Student's reading group (if applicable) ______________________________

Time allotted/day for reading ______________________________

Contingencies ______________________________

Teaching procedures ______________________________

____

____

Observations: ___ None completed for this area

System used:

☐ SECOS ☐ B.O.S.S.

☐ Other ______________________________

Setting of Observations:

☐ ISW: TPsnt ☐ SmGp: Tled ☐ Coop

☐ ISW: TSmGp ☐ LgGp: Tled ☐ Other ______________

SECOS Results:

ISW %	_____	OCA rate	_____
Non ISW %	_____	TA/SW rate	_____
SIC %	_____	TA/OTH rate	_____
AC rate	_____		

B.O.S.S. Results:

AET %	_____	OFT-M%	_____
PET %	_____	OFT-V%	_____
SIC %	_____	OFT-P%	_____
		TDI%	_____

TEACHER-REPORTED STUDENT BEHAVIOR

Rate the following areas from 1 to 5 (1 = very unsatisfactory, 3 = satisfactory, 5 = superior)

Reading Group

a. Oral reading ability (as evidenced in reading group) ____
b. Volunteers answers ____
c. When called upon, gives correct answer ____
d. Attends to other students when they read aloud ____
e. Knows the appropriate place in book ____

Independent Seatwork

a. Stays on task ____
b. Completes assigned work in required time ____
c. Work is accurate ____
d. Works quietly ____
e. Remains in seat when required ____

Homework (if any)

a. Handed in on time ____
b. Is complete ____
c. Is accurate ____

STUDENT-REPORTED BEHAVIOR ____ None completed for this area

Understands expectations of teacher	☐ Yes	☐ No	☐ Not sure
Understands assignments	☐ Yes	☐ No	☐ Not sure
Feels he/she can do the assignments	☐ Yes	☐ No	☐ Not sure
Likes the subject	☐ Yes	☐ No	☐ Not sure
Feels he/she is given enough time to complete assignments	☐ Yes	☐ No	☐ Not sure
Feels he/she is called upon to participate in discussions	☐ Yes	☐ No	☐ Not sure

MATH—SKILLS

Curriculum series used: ____________________

Specific problems in math ____________________

Mastery skill of target student: ____________________

Mastery skill of average student: ____________________

Instructional skill of target student: ____________________

Instructional skill of average student: ____________________

Problems in math applications: ____________________

Probe type	No.	Digits correct/min	Digits incorrect/min	% Problems correct	Learning level (M, I, F)

MATH—ENVIRONMENT

Instructional Procedures

Number of math groups: ______

Student's group (high, middle, low): ______

Allotted time/day: ______

Teaching procedures: ______

______

Contingencies: ______

Observations: ___ None completed for this area

System used:

☐ SECOS ☐ B.O.S.S.

☐ Other ______

Setting of observations:

☐ ISW: TPsnt ☐ SmGp: Tled ☐ Coop

☐ ISW: TSmGp ☐ LgGp: Tled ☐ Other ______

<u>SECOS Results:</u>

ISW % ____ OCA rate ____

Non ISW % ____ TA/SW rate ____

SIC % ____ TA/OTH rate ____

AC rate ____

<u>B.O.S.S. Results:</u>

AET % ____ OFT-M% ____

PET % ____ OFT-V% ____

SIC % ____ OFT-P% ____

TDI% ____

TEACHER REPORTED STUDENT BEHAVIOR

Rate the following areas from 1 to 5 (1 = very unsatisfactory, 3 = satisfactory, 5 = superior)

Math Group (large)

a. Volunteers answers ____
b. When called upon, gives correct answer ____
c. Attends to other students when they give answers ____
d. Knows the appropriate place in math book ____

Math Group (small)

a. Volunteers answers ____
b. When called upon, gives correct answer ____
c. Attends to other students when they give answers ____
d. Knows the appropriate place in math book ____

Math Group (cooperative)

a. Volunteers answers ____
b. Contributes to group objectives ____
c. Attends to other students when they give answers ____
d. Facilitates others in group to participate ____
e. Shows appropriate social skills in group ____

Independent Seatwork

a. Stays on task ____
b. Completes assigned work in required time ____
c. Work is accurate ____
d. Works from initial directions ____
e. Works quietly ____
f. Remains in seat when required ____

Homework (if any)

a. Handed in on time ____
b. Is complete ____
c. Is accurate ____

STUDENT-REPORTED BEHAVIOR ____ None completed for this area

Understands expectations of teacher	☐ Yes	☐ No	☐ Not sure
Understands assignments	☐ Yes	☐ No	☐ Not sure
Feels he/she can do the assignments	☐ Yes	☐ No	☐ Not sure
Likes the subject	☐ Yes	☐ No	☐ Not sure
Feels he/she is given enough time to complete assignments	☐ Yes	☐ No	☐ Not sure
Feels he/she is called upon to participate in discussions	☐ Yes	☐ No	☐ Not sure

SPELLING—SKILLS

Type of material used for spelling instruction:

- ☐ Published spelling series
  Title of series ____________________
- ☐ Basal reading series
  Title of series ____________________
- ☐ Teacher-made materials
- ☐ Other ____________________

Curriculum series (if applicable): ____________________

Results of Spelling Probes:

Grade level of probe	Probe #	LSC/min	% Words Correct	Median LSC for Grade level	Level (M, I, F)
	1				
	2				
	3				
	1				
	2				
	3				
	1				
	2				
	3				
	1				
	2				
	3				

SPELLING—ENVIRONMENT

Instructional Procedures

Time allotted/day for reading ____________________

Teaching procedures: ____________________

Contingencies: ____________________

Observations: ___ None completed for this area

System used:

☐ SECOS ☐ B.O.S.S.

☐ Other ________________________

Setting of Observations:

☐ ISW: TPsnt ☐ SmGp: Tled ☐ Coop

☐ ISW: TSmGp ☐ LgGp: Tled ☐ Other ____________

SECOS Results:

ISW %	_____	OCA rate	_____
Non ISW %	_____	TA/SW rate	_____
SIC %	_____	TA/OTH rate	_____
AC rate	_____		

B.O.S.S. Results:

AET %	_____	OFT-M%	_____
PET %	_____	OFT-V%	_____
		OFT-P%	_____
		TDI%	_____

STUDENT-REPORTED BEHAVIOR _____ None completed for this area

Understands expectations of teacher	☐ Yes	☐ No	☐ Not sure
Understands assignments	☐ Yes	☐ No	☐ Not sure
Feels he/she can do the assignments	☐ Yes	☐ No	☐ Not sure
Likes the subject	☐ Yes	☐ No	☐ Not sure
Feels he/she is given enough time to complete assignments	☐ Yes	☐ No	☐ Not sure
Feels he/she is called upon to participate in discussions	☐ Yes	☐ No	☐ Not sure

WRITING—SKILLS

Types of writing assignments: ________________________________

Areas of difficulty:

Content:

☐ Expressing thoughts
☐ Story length
☐ Story depth
☐ Creativity

Mechanics:

☐ Capitalization
☐ Punctuation
☐ Grammar
☐ Handwriting
☐ Spelling

Results of Written Expression Probes:

Story starter	Words written/ 3 min	Instructional level	Comments

WRITING—ENVIRONMENT

Instructional Procedures

Allotted time/day ______________________________

Teaching procedures: ______________________________

____

Observations: ___ None completed for this area

System used:

☐ SECOS ☐ B.O.S.S.

☐ Other ______________________

Setting of Observations:

☐ ISW: TPsnt ☐ SmGp: Tled ☐ Coop

☐ ISW: TSmGp ☐ LgGp: Tled ☐ Other ____________

<u>SECOS Results:</u>

ISW % _____ OCA rate _____

Non ISW % _____ TA/SW rate _____

SIC % _____ TA/OTH rate _____

AC rate _____

<u>B.O.S.S. Results:</u>

AET % _____ OFT-M% _____

PET % _____ OFT-V% _____

OFT-P% _____

TDI% _____

STUDENT-REPORTED BEHAVIOR _____ None completed for this area

Understands expectations of teacher	☐ Yes	☐ No	☐ Not sure
Understands assignments	☐ Yes	☐ No	☐ Not sure
Feels he/she can do the assignments	☐ Yes	☐ No	☐ Not sure
Likes the subject	☐ Yes	☐ No	☐ Not sure
Feels he/she is given enough time to complete assignments	☐ Yes	☐ No	☐ Not sure
Feels he/she is called upon to participate in discussions	☐ Yes	☐ No	☐ Not sure

STEP 3

Instructional Modification

The Folding-In Technique

The "folding-in" technique has been found to be a powerful and easy-to-implement strategy that can be useful in any intervention whose objective is for a student to acquire new, fact-based information. The intervention can cut across subjects and can be used for anything from teaching students letter recognition in kindergarten, to word recognition, to multiplication facts, to events leading up to the Civil War, to chemical formulas.

Based upon the suggested ratios of Gickling's model of curriculum-based assessment (Gickling & Havertape, 1981), the procedure attempts to build success and momentum for acquisition of new information. By assessing a student's entry knowledge of the skill to be learned, the evaluator can determine the material a student already knows and the material that is unknown. When the new material is taught, the ratio of known to unknown material is maintained at no greater than 70% known to 30% unknown. Thus, a student who is being exposed to new material is never asked to try to learn more than 30% of what is presented.

The folding-in technique is based in part upon findings about the amount of repetition a student needs in order to master new information (Hargis, Terhaar-Yonkers, Williams, & Reed, 1988). Learning is conceptualized as a process described in Figure 13 . In the acquisition stage, a student begins to be exposed to new material; in the mastery stage, the student becomes fluent with the material; and in the generalization and adaptation stages, the student discovers ways of applying the same or similar knowledge to novel situations. At an IQ level of 100, it takes approximately 35 repetitions to move from a level of acquisition to mastery. As the IQ goes up to 115, the number of repetitions decreases to about 15. At an IQ of 85, the number of repetitions increases to about 55 (Gates, 1930). The folding-in technique is designed to maximize the number of repetitions of new material within a short period of time, thereby facilitating the student's progress from the acquisition to the mastery level of learning.

Level	Emphasis	Strategies
Acquisition	Achieving accurate responding	Demonstration, modeling, cues, prompting
Mastery	Accuracy with speed	Routine and novel drill and practice
Generalization	Performance and response under novel stimuli	Training discrimination and differentiation
Adaptation	Performance of similar reponses under novel stimuli	Problem solving, role playing, training under simulation conditions

FIGURE 13. Stages of the learning process.

To illustrate the technique, it is described in detail for use in teaching word recognition and reading fluency, and acquisition of multiplication facts within a peer-tutoring context. Again, it is important for the reader to recognize that the technique can be applied to any content area where fact-based knowledge needs to be learned.

EXAMPLE: FOLDING-IN TECHNIQUE FOR WORD ACQUISITION AND READING FLUENCY

Step 1: The evaluator selects a passage for the student to read. The passage should be one that the student is currently working on in class. It is important that the passage contain no more than 50% unknown material. This can be assessed by conducting a word search: The evaluator simply asks the student to read and explain the meaning of various key words from the passage. If the student misses more than 50% of the words in the word search, the evaluator should select a different passage and repeat the process.

Step 2: The evaluator asks the student to read a portion of the passage (usually a paragraph or two) aloud, and times the reading. The evaluator marks the point in the passage reached by the student at the end of 1 minute. The number of words read correctly in this minute is designated as the presession reading fluency.

Step 3: As the student reads, the evaluator notes at least three words that the student has difficulty with or doesn't seem to understand. On 3 × 5 index cards, the evaluator writes the three words (one on each card). These words are designated as "unknowns." If there are more than three words that can be designated as unknown, the evaluator selects words that are meaningful and help the student to understand the story.

Step 4: On 3 x 5 index cards, the evaluator writes 7 words (one on each card) from the passage that the student does seem to know. These should be words that are meaningful to the passage, not simply "and," "the," or other nonmeaningful expressions.

Step 5: The session begins with presentation of the first unknown word. The evaluator should define the word for the student and use it in a sentence. Next, the evaluator should ask the student to repeat the definition and use it in a different sentence.

Step 6: Now the folding-in begins. After the unknown word is presented, one of the known words is presented. The student is asked to say the word aloud. Next, the unknown word is again presented, followed by the known word previously presented, and then a new known word. This sequence of presentation (unknown followed by knowns) is continued until all 7 knowns and the 1 unknown word have been presented.

Next, the second unknown word is presented. The word is presented in the same way as the first, with first the evaluator and then the student defining it and using it in a sentence. This second unknown word is then folded in among the other 7 known words and 1 unknown word. In the course of the multiple presentations of the words, the student is asked to repeat the unknown word's definition and to use it in a sentence whenever he/she hesitates or is incorrect in the pronunciation of the word. Finally, the third unknown is folded in among the other 9 words (2 unknown, 7 known). Given that the other words were assessed to be known at the starting point, the student should not have any difficulty with these words. Figure 14 illustrates the full sequence of presentations for a set of 10 words.

Step 7: Upon completion of the folding-in intervention, the student is asked to reread the passage. The evaluator marks the number of seconds it took for the student to reach the point in the passage reached at 1 minute during the presession reading. It is important that the student read at least to the same point of the passage that he/she reached at the beginning of the session; this is necessary to establish accuracy in the oral-reading rate measure. The score obtained here is considered the student's postsession reading score.

Step 8: Both the pre- and postsession scores are graphed (usually by the student). These data can be very useful in showing the student the consistent improvement in his/her reading skills over the short period of time in each session, as well as the acquisition of material over days and weeks.

Step 9: The next session begins by having the student read the next portion of the passage. Following the reading, the 10 words (7 known, 3 unknown) that were used in the previous session are reviewed. A mark is placed on one of the unknown words to designate that the student knows the word without hesitation during this session.

Step 10: A criterion is set to determine when a previously unknown word is designated as a known word. Typically, this may be defined as getting the word correct in two consecutive sessions after it has been introduced.

Step 11: As a new unknown word is added to the drill procedure, one of the original known words is removed from the pile. The first word to be removed is one of

Presentation #	Unknown Item #	Known Item #
1	1	
2		1
3	1	
4		1
5		2
6	1	
7		1
8		2
9		3
10	1	
11		1
12		2
13		3
14		4
15	1	
16		1
17		2
18		3
19		4
20		5
21	1	
22		1
23		2
24		3
25		4
26		5
27		6
28	1	
29		1
30		2
31		3
32		4
33		5
34		6
35		7
36	2	
37	1	
38		1
39	2	
40	1	
41		1
42		2
43		3
44	2	
45	1	
46		1
47		2
48		3
49		4
50	2	
51	1	
52		1
53		2
54		3
55		4
56		5
57	2	
58	1	
59		1
60		2
61		3
62		4

FIGURE 14. Sequences for presenting known and unknown materials in the folding-in technique, assuming 10 items (3 unknown and 7 known).

Presenta-tion #	Unknown Item #	Known Item #
63		5
64		6
65	2	
66	1	
67		1
68		2
69		3
70		4
71		5
72		6
73		7
74	3	
75	2	
76	1	
77		1
78	3	
79	2	
80	1	
81		1
82		2
83	3	

Presenta-tion #	Unknown Item #	Known Item #
84	2	
85	1	
86		1
87		2
88		3
89	3	
90	2	
91	1	
92		1
93		2
94		3
95		4
96	3	
97	2	
98	1	
99		1
100		2
101		3
102		4
103		5
104	3	
105	2	

Presenta-tion #	Unknown Item #	Known Item #
106	1	
107		1
108		2
109		3
110		4
111		5
112		6
113	3	
114	2	
115	1	
116		1
117		2
118		3
119		4
120		5
121		6
122		7

FIGURE 14 *continued*

the original known words selected on the first session. Each of the other 7 known words is gradually replaced with new unknown words. Finally, by the time one of the original unknown words is removed from the pile, it will have been drilled far in excess of the required 55 repetitions for new material to reach mastery levels.

EXAMPLE: FOLDING-IN TECHNIQUE FOR MULTIPLICATION FACTS

Students: Two boys in third-grade special education class. Both boys have been referred for problems in learning multiplication facts.

Preassessment Phase: To determine the number of known and unknown facts, the students are administered a quiz in which they are asked to answer all computational problems with fact families 1 through 9. The number of problems not completed or incorrect provides an indication of the facts that have been and have not been learned.

Instructional Structure: The procedure is set up as a peer-tutoring activity. The students are taught the procedure and required to conduct 10-minute tutoring sessions in which they drill each other using the folding-in technique.

Step 1: Each student selects seven cards from his pile of preassessed known facts.

Step 2: Each student selects one card from his unknown pile of preassessed facts.

Step 3: The two students are informed by the teacher that they have 20 minutes to begin tutoring.

Step 4: After it is decided which student will begin the tutoring, the folding-in procedure begins. The teacher of the pair presents the first unknown fact to the learner. The learner is required to write the fact on a piece of paper, say it to himself three times, and then turn the paper over.

Step 5: The teacher than presents a known fact, followed by the unknown fact, the first known fact, and another known fact. The unknown fact is presented sequentially in this fashion until all 7 known facts have been presented and folded in with the unknown fact. (See Figure 14 for presentation sequence.)

Step 6: The group of 8 facts (1 unknown and 7 unknown) are shuffled. The second unknown fact is then presented and folded in among the other 8 facts. This is repeated again for the third unknown fact.

Step 7: If a student hesitates or is incorrect on any fact, the teacher instructs the student to complete a brief correction procedure. The teacher tells the learner the correct answer and has the learner write the incorrect fact three times. The incorrect fact is then presented again to the learner.

Step 8: When all facts have been folded in, the entire group of 10 facts is presented three times. Each time, the packet of index cards is shuffled to prevent the learner from simply remembering the sequence of responses.

Step 9: The final step is a test of the 10 facts that the students have practiced. On this test, a mark is placed on each unknown-fact card if a student is correct on this trial. When an unknown fact attains three consecutive marks, it is considered a learned fact.

Step 10: The number of new facts learned each week is graphed by the students. In addition, the teacher administers weekly curriculum-based measurement math probes taken from across all fact families. These data are also graphed.

STEP 4

Progress Monitoring

♦♦♦

Graphing Data

♦

One of the key components of progress monitoring is providing a visual display of the outcomes of the data collection process. Such graphic displays serve to improve the evaluator's own understanding of the data; they also offer an effective mechanism for communicating with parents, teachers, and students themselves about the students' progress. Indeed, the process of collecting and reporting the data in a graphic form can itself serve as a strong motivator and reinforcer for some students.

SETTING UP GRAPHIC DISPLAYS

Graphic displays of data are useful for both short- and long-term monitoring. The setting-up process is similar for all types of graphs:

Step 1: Identify the metric that is being used for data collection purposes. This can be words correct or incorrect per minute, cumulative problems learned, number of pages mastered, number of homework problems done correctly, or other such measures.

Step 2: Identify the possible range that the metric used for data collection can occupy. This can be any set of numbers representing the lower and upper limits that the measure is likely to attain.

Step 3: The metric used for data collection becomes the range placed on the *y* (vertical) axis. Divide the range into equal units and write these along the vertical axis.

Step 4: Identify the amount of time across which the data will be collected. This can be any unit of time up to a full school year.

Step 5: The amount of time for data collection becomes the range placed on the x (horizontal) axis. Divide the range into equal units (sessions, days, weeks, months, etc.).

The data are plotted by placing points on the graph, each of which indicates the outcome on the measure used for monitoring at each point in time when data are collected.

Graphs are usually divided by the particular phase of the intervention. Data obtained during baseline and intervention phases are separated by a solid line drawn on the graph. The data are also not connected by lines across these two phases. Once the intervention begins, changes in the intervention procedure are designated by broken lines, with the data again not being connected through those phases.

Figure 15 shows a graphic display for a first-grade student for whom two interventions, peer-tutoring and peer tutoring plus curriculum-based measurement (CBM) feedback, were implemented to improve acquisition of basic math facts in addition and subtraction. The intervention took place for 15 weeks (one semester). Baseline and intervention phases are separated by a solid line, and the two intervention phases are separated by a broken line.

INTERPRETING GRAPHIC DATA

Deciding whether the data collected over time indicate that outcomes are moving in the expected direction can be done in several ways. Two of the most common methods of trend analysis are the quarter-intersect or split-middle method of White and Haring (1980), and the more mathematically precise method of calculating an ordinary least squares (OLS) trend line.

Quarter-Intersect (or Split-Middle) Method

To illustrate the first method of trend estimation, a step-by-step example is provided.

Figure 16A displays the data from the peer-tutoring phase (see Figure 15) of the intervention program described above, designed to improve the math computation performance of a first-grade student. To calculate a trend estimation, the following is done:

Step 1: Divide the entire data series of interest into two equal parts. If the number of data points is odd, than the middle data point of the series becomes the dividing line. If the number of data points is even, than the data series are split between the two middle points of the data series. In this example, there are 16 data points, so the series is split between the 8th and 9th data points of the series. (See Figure 16B.)

Step 2: Find the median score for each of the two sets of the data series. The median score is the middle or central score among the data points. If the middle score

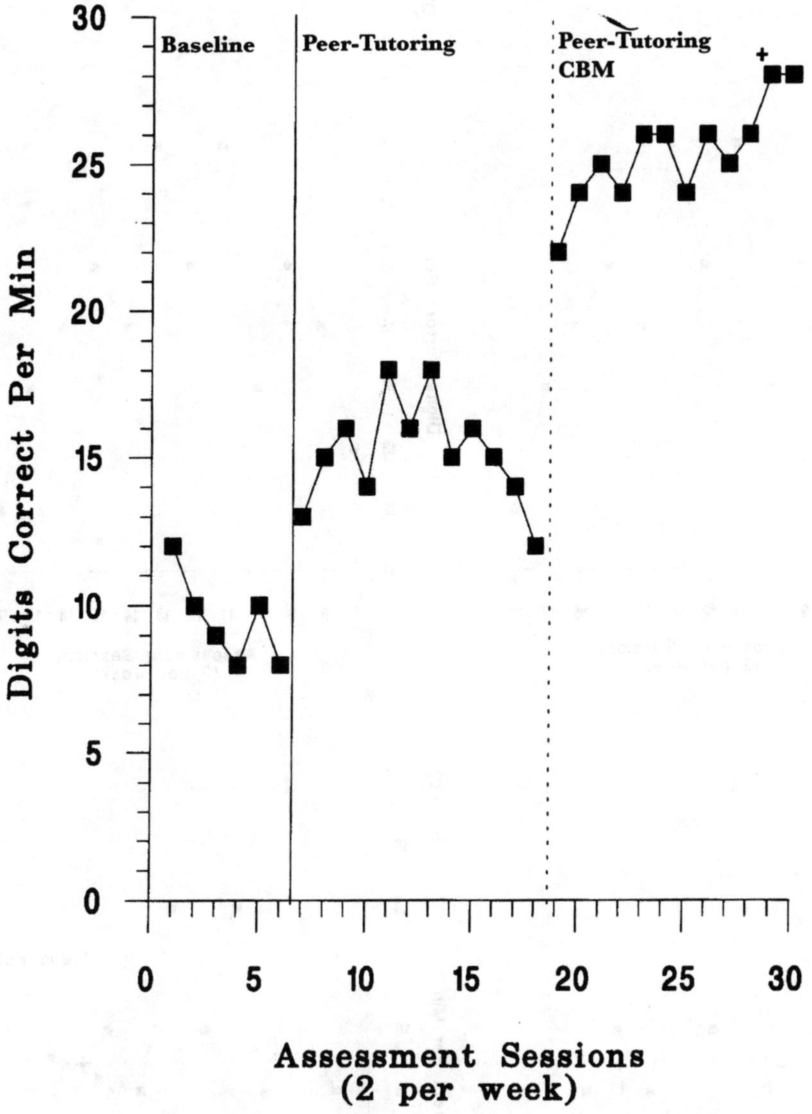

FIGURE 15. Graphic display of two interventions implemented to improve math performance.

falls between two data points, than the median score is the halfway point between these two scores. In this example, there are 8 data points in each half of the series. An examination of the data in the left half of the series shows that the score of 15.5 is the median score. The score for the right half of the data series is 15.5. (See Figure 16C.)

Step 3: Connect the median scores for each half of the data series. (See Figure 16D.) This line represents the trend estimation for the data series.

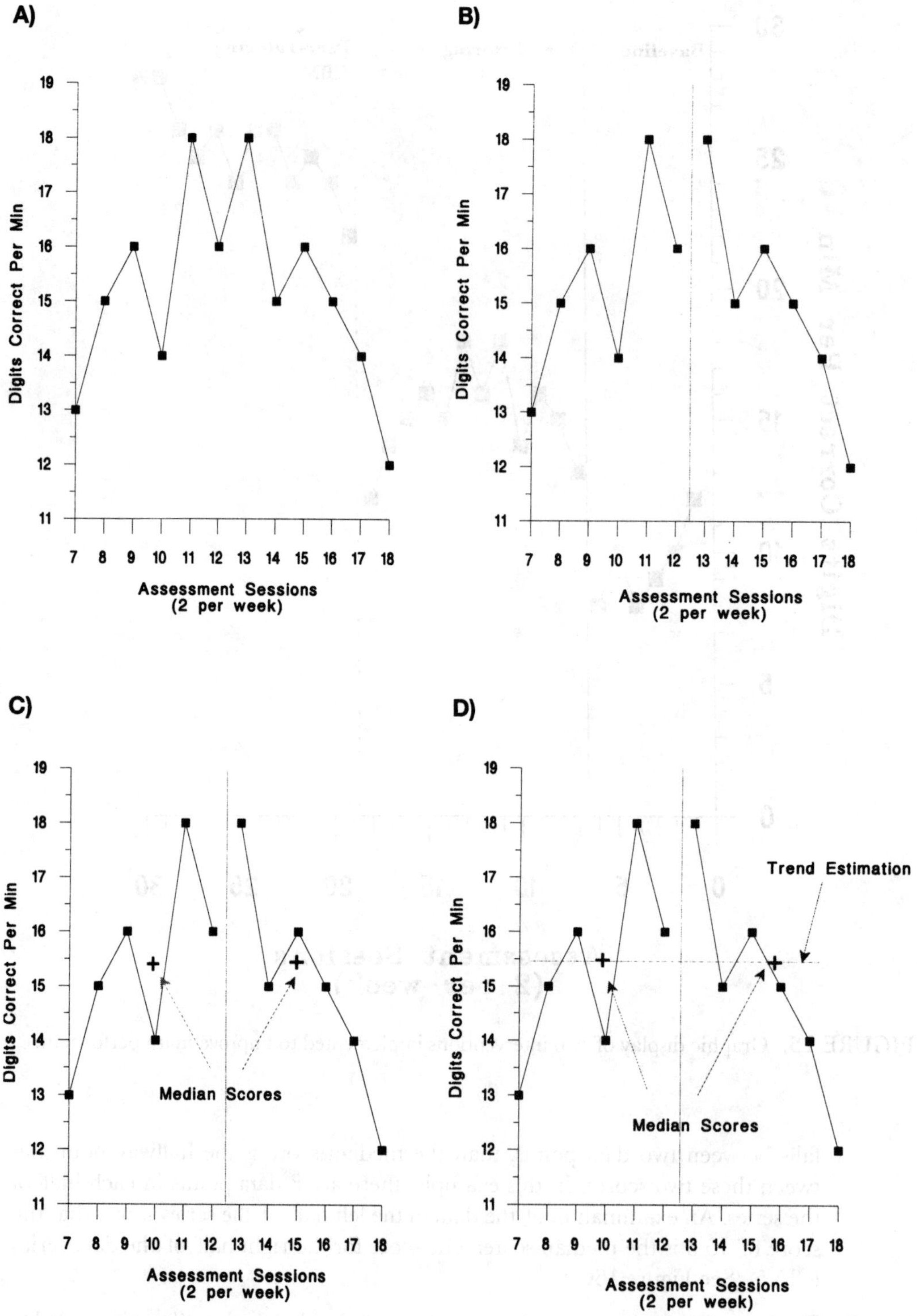

FIGURE 16. Illustration of the quarter-intersect or split-middle method of trend estimation for the peer-tutoring phase displayed in Figure 15.

Ordinary Least Squares (OLS) Method

The OLS method is the generation of a regression of the data points to a line that best fits the data series. Although OLS can be mathematically complex to calculate, the use of computers make this measure simple to generate. Almost all graphic software products, such as Microsoft Excel, Quarto-pro, or Harvard Graphics, contain a function within the program that will allow OLS to be calculated. If one does not have access to these programs, the calculation of OLS can become problematic.

In practice, it is recommended that the OLS method be used if it can be obtained, since research has shown it to be more accurate than other trend line estimation methods, such as the quarter-intersect method. Figure 17 shows the results of OLS calculated for the same data set as that used for the quarter-intersect method in Figure 16.

PREPARING CURRICULUM-BASED MEASUREMENT (CBM) GRAPHS

The use of CBM requires that specific types of graphs be generated. These graphs provide opportunities to collect data across a long period of time (usually an entire school

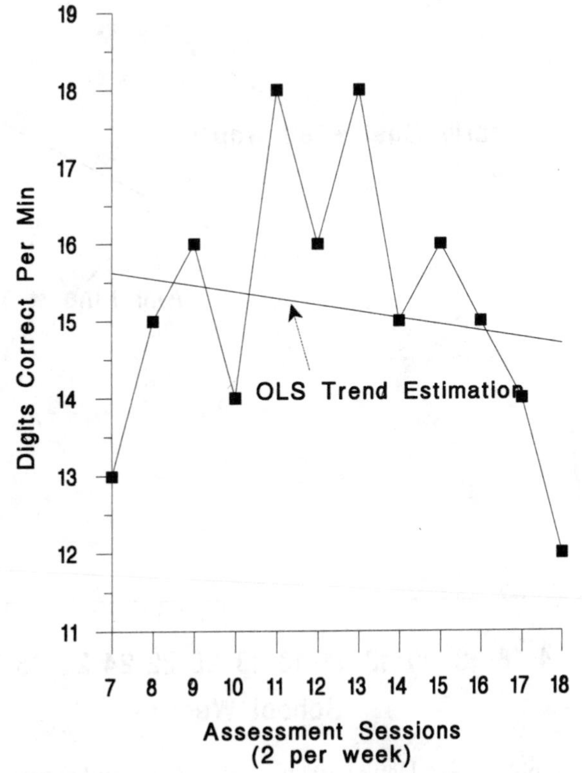

FIGURE 17. Illustration of the ordinary least squares (OLS) method of trend estimation for the peer-tutoring phase displayed in Figure 15.

year), and to incorporate goal setting and graphing of expected performance. For example, Dan is a beginning third-grade student. Baseline data taken over 3 days show that Dan is reading at 48 words correct per minute (wcpm), 30 wcpm, and 53 wcpm in third-grade material. Using scores collected during a local norming project of Dan's school district, the teacher elects to set a yearly goal for Dan to read at the 50th percentile of third-grade readers by the end of the year—that is, a goal of 90 wcpm. Figure 18 shows the CBM graph generated from these data. In the figure, Dan's baseline is represented by the median score across the three baseline data sessions (48 wcpm). A goal of 90 wcpm at the end of a 36-week period (1 academic year from the time the data collection is started in September) is indicated on the graph, and a solid line connecting the baseline and goal is drawn. This line represents Dan's "aim line." As data are collected over time, it is anticipated that his performance will match this line of progress. If his scores consistently exceed the aim line, than the teacher may decide to increase the goal originally set for Dan. If his scores are consistently below the aim line or move in a direction opposite to that

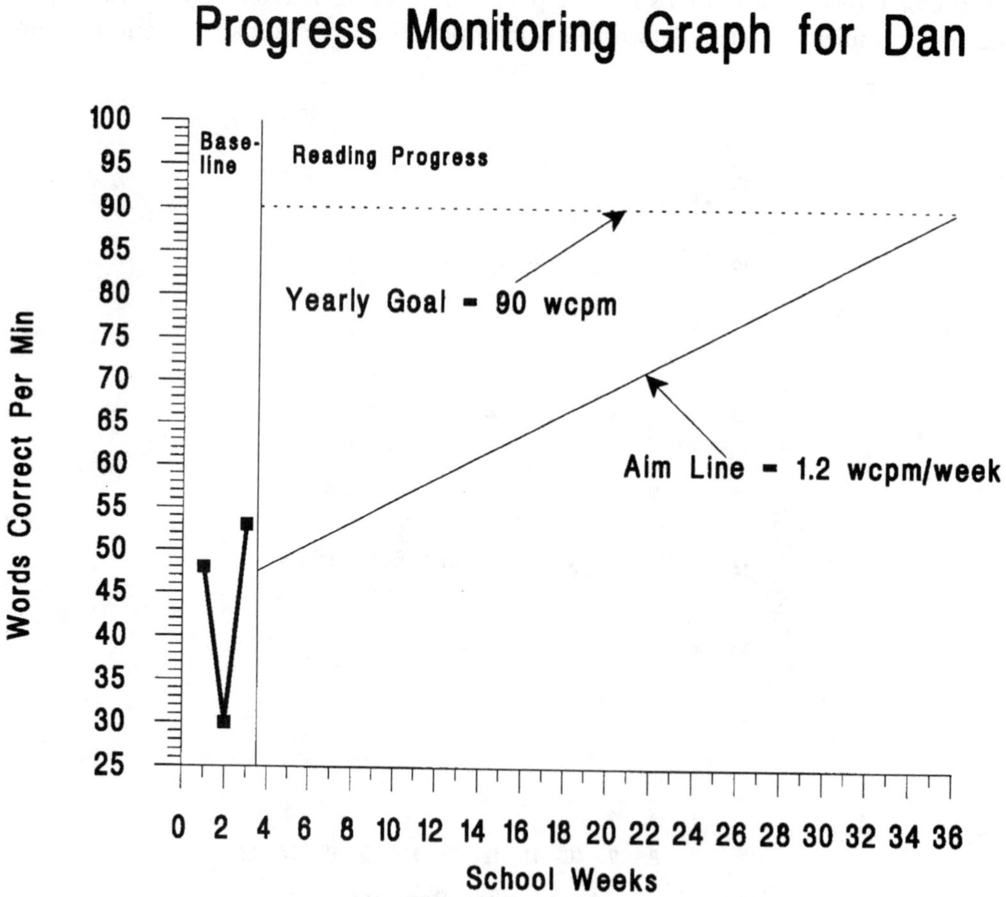

FIGURE 18. CBM graph showing Dan's baseline performance and expected rate of progress in reading across a school year.

shown by the aim line, the teacher should decide to alter the instructional technique to improve Dan's performance. Also, with the goal of 90 wcpm, Dan is expected to improve his oral reading fluency by 1.2 wcpm each week; this is his "slope" of expected improvement (90 wcpm – 48 wcpm = 42 wcpm ÷ 36 weeks = 1.2 wcpm/week). Exercise 12 provides an opportunity to practice developing a CBM graph.

Exercise 12: Developing a CBM Graph

Student

Betsy is a beginning fourth-grader. Her reading fluency at baseline is determined to be 40 wcpm in fourth-grade material, where she will be taught this year. Her teacher, looking to set a goal that places Betsy at least at the 25th percentile for fourth-graders at the end of the year, selects 88 wcpm as her year-end goal. Biweekly monitoring of her reading performance is planned across the 35 weeks of the school year.

Data

During the first 5 weeks of school, the teacher obtains the following data:

Week 1: 45 wcpm
35 wcpm

Week 2: 50 wcpm
46 wcpm

Week 3: 50 wcpm
44 wcpm

Week 4: 48 wcpm
56 wcpm

Week 5: 52 wcpm
55 wcpm

Instructions

1. Construct a graph including an aim line.
2. Plot Betsy's actual performance.
3. Use the quarter-intersect method to plot a trend estimation for Betsy's performance.
4. What might be the teacher's decision, based on these data?

Progress Monitoring Graph in Reading for Betsy

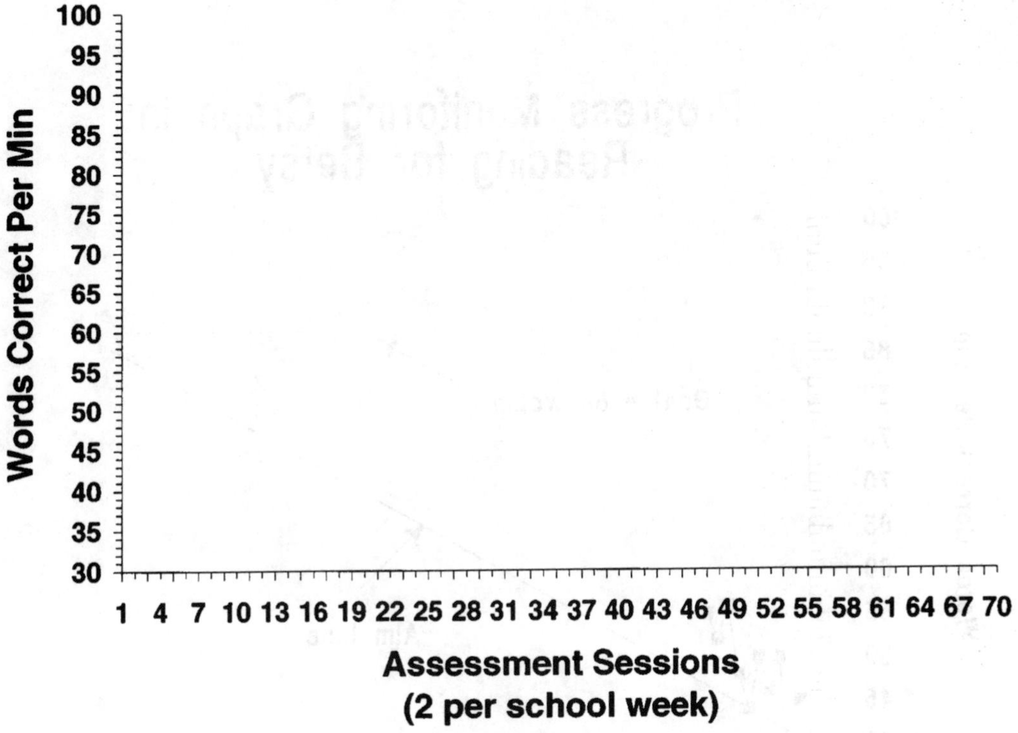

Answers for Exercise 12: Developing a Graph

The results of graphing Betsy's performance are shown in Figure 19. A trend line using the quarter-intersect method, shown in Figure 20, indicates that Betsy is making greater progress than would be expected. As such, it is possible that the goal set for her is currently too low. The teacher may decide to reset the goal for Betsy at 98 wcpm rather than 88. When the new goal line is drawn, a dashed vertical line is drawn on the graph, and the new aim line using a goal of 98 wcpm from the starting point (the baseline of 40 wcpm) is drawn. Figure 21 shows the resulting CBM graph with the increased goal.

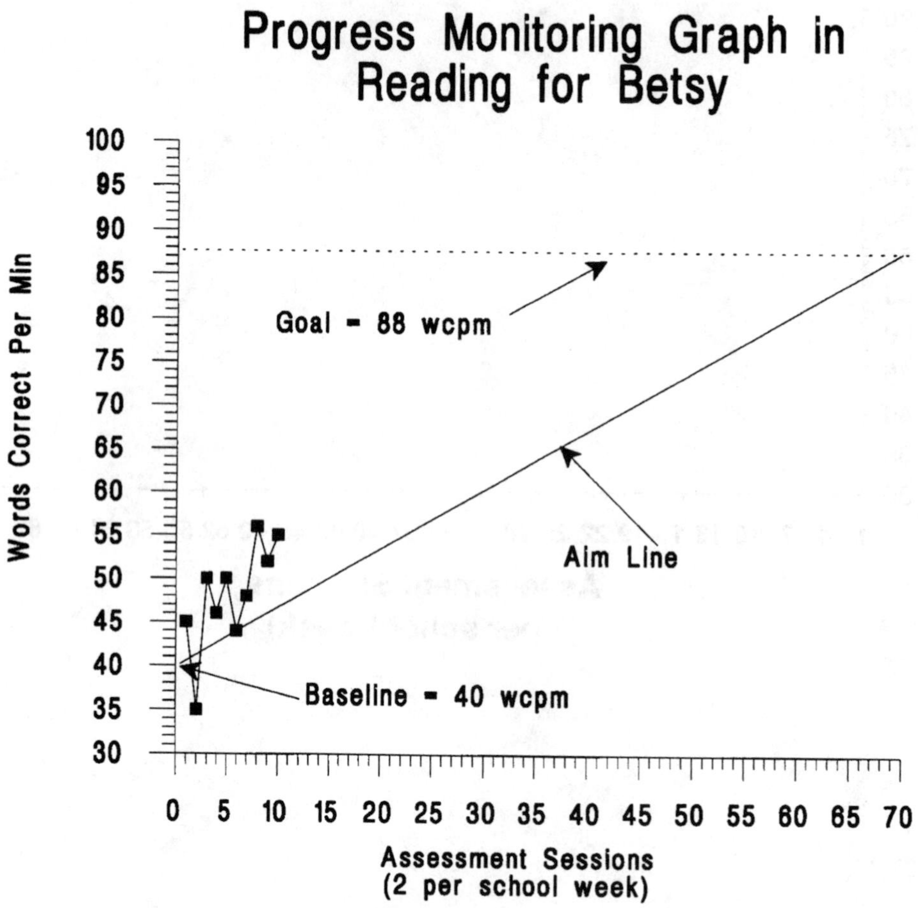

FIGURE 19. Betsy's CBM graph.

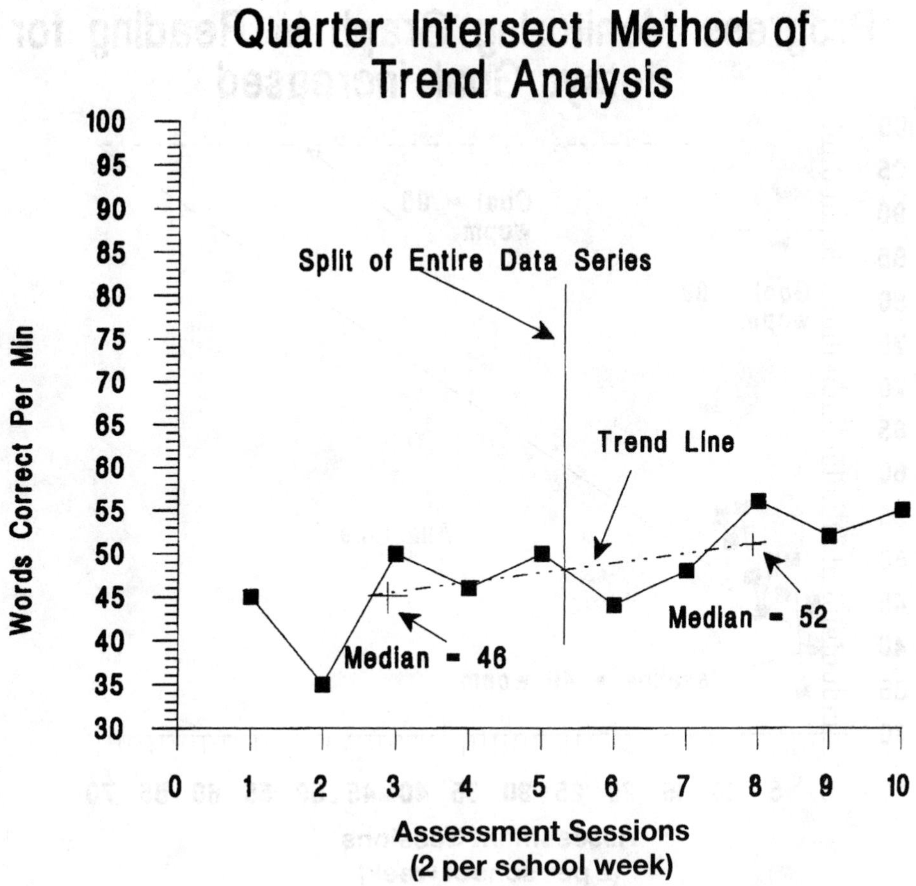

FIGURE 20. Quarter-intersect trend estimation for Betsy's progress.

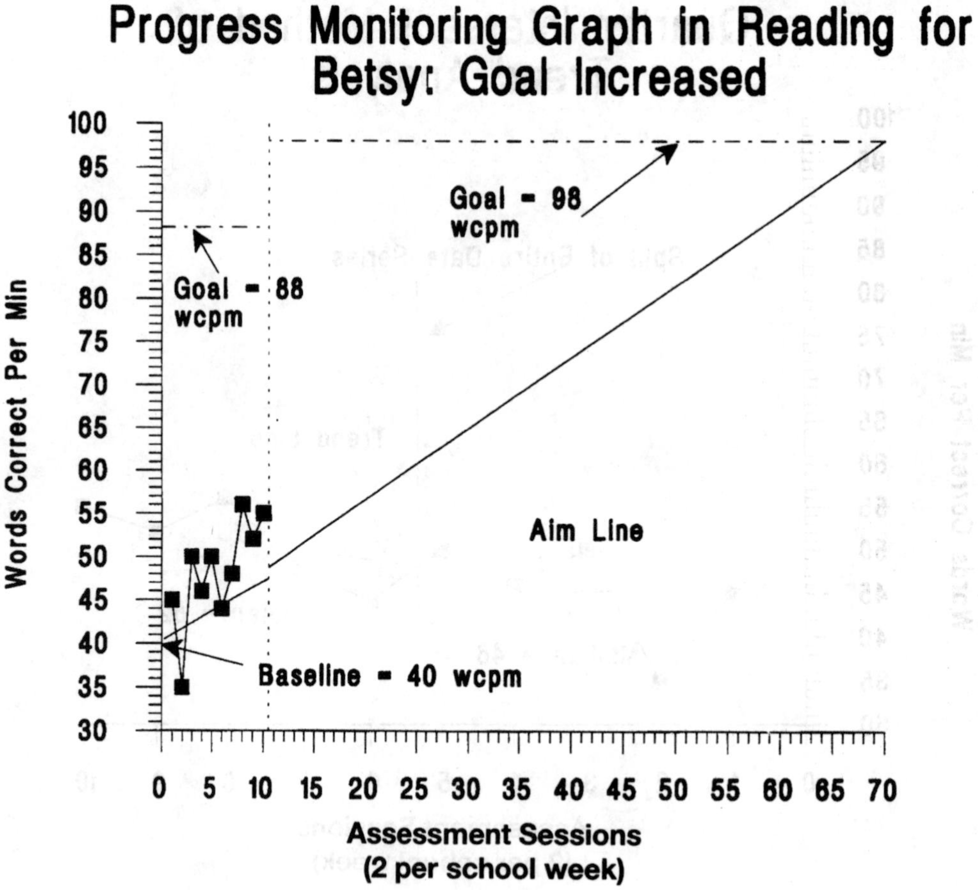

FIGURE 21. Betsy's CBM graph wih increased goal.

♦♦♦

Developing Local Norms

♦

The process of selecting goals in curriculum-based assessment can be greatly enhanced by the use of local norms. Shinn (1988, 1989) provides an excellent discussion of this process, and offers step-by-step directions on how to construct these norms. Specifically, Shinn (1988) notes that one must create a measurement net that defines the appropriate skills and materials for assessment; establish a normative sampling plan; train data collectors; have the data collected; and summarize the data. Gathering data that represent the performance of students within the schools where the data will be used provides a strong sense of the ownership of the outcomes, and increases the certainty that the data comparison will be representative of the community.

To illustrate this process, the steps involved in the collection of local norms in reading for elementary school students from a medium-sized, urban school district are described. The reader should note that the sampling procedures used here are different from those recommended by Shinn (1988).

CREATING THE MEASUREMENT NET

The school district was using a Houghton Mifflin (1986) basal reading program. Data were to be collected three times during the year: fall (October), winter (February), and spring (May). Reading levels of average students within grades were inconsistent across the district. At some schools, students were reading at levels commensurate with the publisher's assessment of grade level of the material; in other schools, the majority of students were reading approximately one level (or book) behind. When this discrepancy was discussed with the school district, it was decided to use the publisher-recommended grade level materials as the measures to be assessed. Passages for assessment were taken from materials that constituted the end-of-year goals for students in each grade.

Grade	Name of Book	Publisher's Assigned Grade Level
1	*Parades*	Primer
2	*Discoveries*	2:2*
3	*Journeys*	3:2*
4	*Flights*	4
5	*Expectations*	5

*Indicates second book of grade level.

Randomly selected passages of between 150 and 200 words were selected from each book, according to standard CBM procedures. Passages were retyped on separate pages for presentation.

SELECTING THE SAMPLE

Given the size of the school district and resources available for data collection, it was not possible simply to select students randomly from across the district, as is often recommended in the process of obtaining local norms. In addition, the school district included a wide range of socioeconomic and academic ability levels, which needed to be equally represented in the sample.

To address the problems of the resources available to collect the data, it was decided to concentrate the normative sample on three elementary schools. In considering the wide range of socioeconomic levels, the school district administrators identified three schools that represented lower (L), lower middle (LM), and middle (M) socioeconomic levels (the three levels most characteristic of the district). To validate the selection of these schools, the percentages of students on free or reduced-fee lunches in the three schools were compared. The L school had 93% of the students on free or reduced-fee lunches; the LM school had 56%; and the M school had 23%. Thus, these three schools appeared to accurately represent the range of socioeconomic levels in the district.

The next problem was to develop a sample that would fairly represent the range of reading abilities within each of these schools. To accomplish this, prior to each scheduled assessment, the reading specialist assigned to each school provided a list of the current placement within the reading series of all students in that building. These data were used to identify the proportion of students in each grade within a building at each level of the reading series. For example, in the L building, it was found that in the third grade 10% of the students were reading in *Flights* (the fourth-grade book), 30% were reading in *Journeys* (the second book of the third grade), 40% were reading in *Caravans* (the first book of the third grade), 15% were reading in *Discoveries* (the second book of the second grade), and 5% were reading in *Adventures* (the first book of the second grade).

A normative sample consisting of a total of 450 students was developed, representing approximately 25% of the population of the three schools. From each school, 150 students (30 per grade) were selected. The normative sample within each school was constructed by selecting the identical proportion of students from each level of the reading series within each grade within each school. For example, to select the students from the third grade in the L school, the list of students placed in the *Discoveries* book was obtained. As noted above, this represented 15% of the third-grade students. Given that the final sample from the third grade of the L school would have 30 students, a total of 4 (15% of 30) would be selected at random from among the possible 15% for inclusion in the normative sample. This process was repeated for each grade level and each school, in order to end up with a final sample whose representation was proportional to the percentage of students at the various reading levels of the grade.

DATA COLLECTION

Data were collected over 2-week periods in October, February, and May of the 1990–1991 school year. Graduate students in school psychology and special education served as data collectors. Students were tested on an individual basis in a small room adjacent to the classrooms in each of the school buildings. Each student was asked to read a passage aloud and timed for 1-minute. The number of words read correctly per minute was calculated according to standard CBM techniques. Errors included mispronunciations, omissions, and substitutions.

DATA ANALYSIS AND RESULTS

Results obtained from the normative data collection can be displayed in numerous ways. Figures 22 and 23 show the overall outcomes for the entire district. Such data as these can be used as the benchmarks for a district's expectations and performance.

The data can also be broken down by individual schools. Figure 24 shows the mean performance levels across the three schools. Examination of these data show that average student performance across the schools within the district were quite different. For example, in the third grade, it was found that the mean performance of students from the L and LM schools was about 30–40% lower than the performance of students in the M school. After third grade, these differences lessened. Still, the data show that throughout all grades and assessments across the school year, reading performance was clearly differentiated by the school a student attended. Thus, a student reading at the 50th percentile of the L school was often near the 25th percentile of the M school. Such data may be useful in helping teachers within schools predict expected levels of performance; they may also assist administrators in setting school-wide goals for reading performance.

Grade	Percentile	Fall	Winter	Spring
1	25th	1	6	16
	50th	4	15	48
	75th	7	24	80
2	25th	18	27	42
	50th	39	59	77
	75th	59	91	111
3	25th	40	50	61
	50th	62	76	87
	75th	84	102	112
4	25th	66	80	88
	50th	85	102	112
	75th	104	124	135
5	25th	78	88	97
	50th	104	116	129
	75th	129	147	160

FIGURE 22. Quartiles for local norms in reading from grade level basal reading materials for a medium-sized metropolitan school district in the northeastern United States.

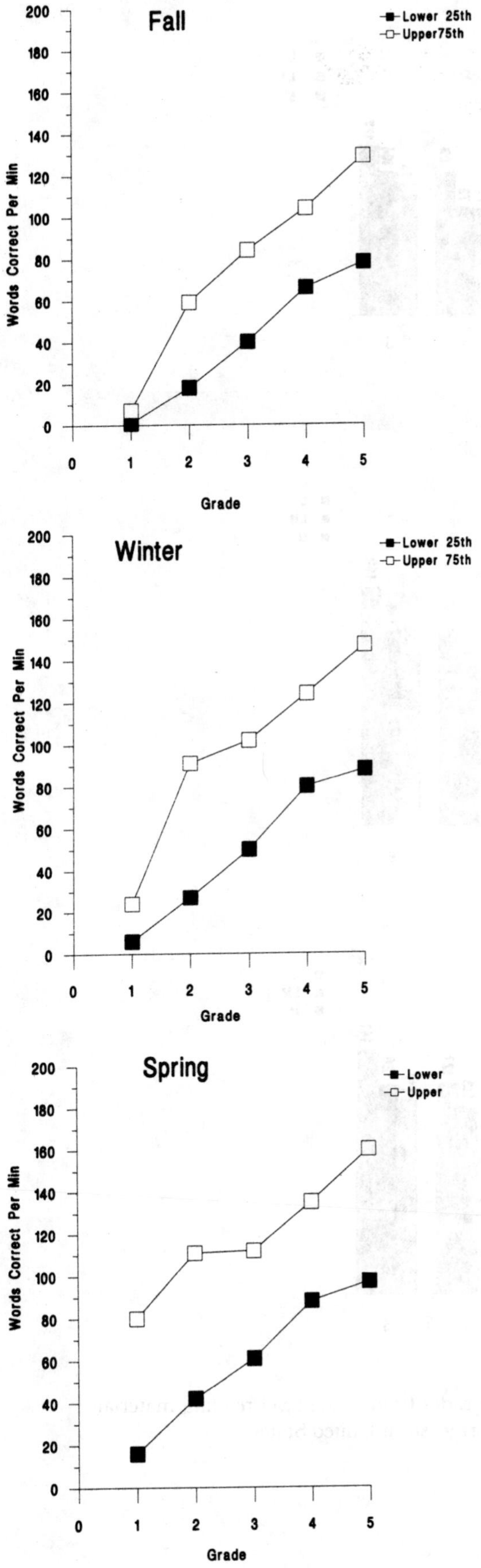

FIGURE 23. Graphic depiction of the range of performance across grades from grade level reading materials for a medium-sized metropolitan school district in the northeastern United States.

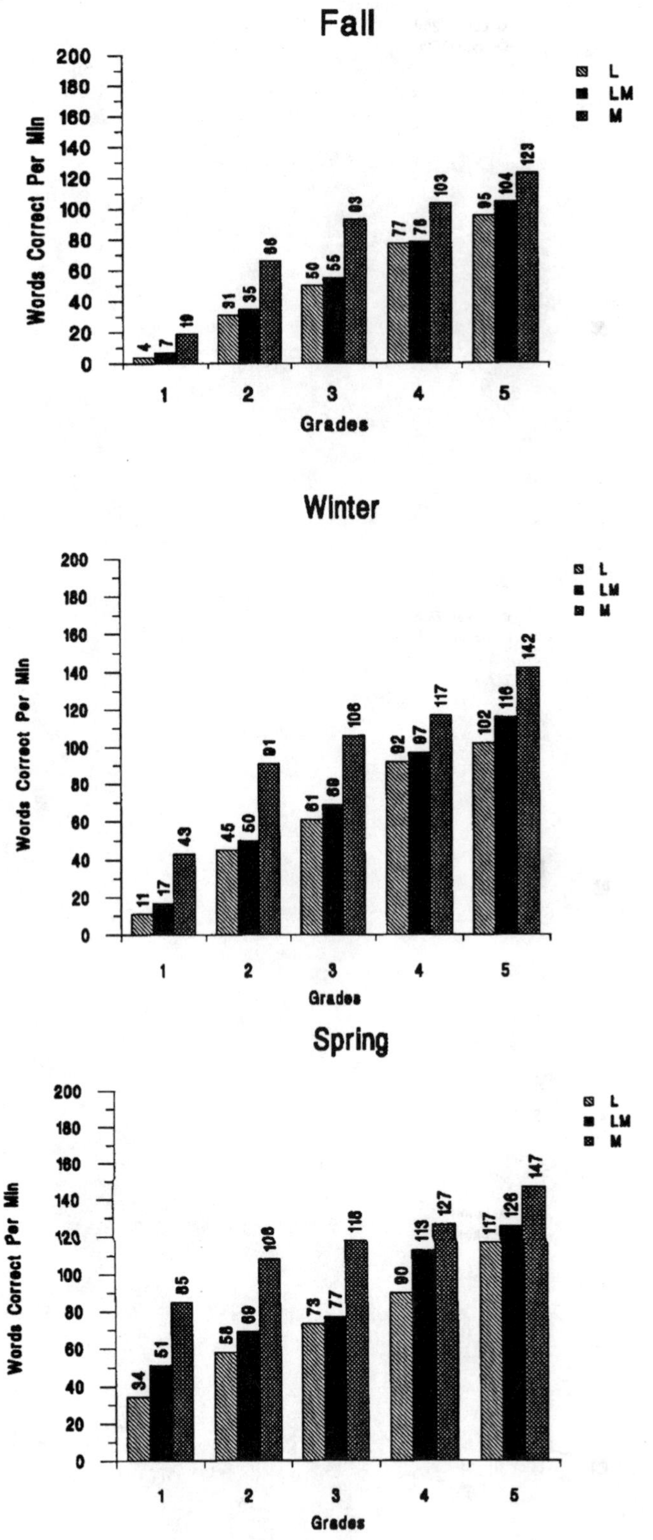

FIGURE 24. Mean performance across schools and grades from grade level reading materials for a medium-sized metropolitan school district in the northeastern United States.

References

DuPaul, G. J., Rapport, M. D., & Perriello, L. M. (1991). Teacher ratings of academic skills: The development of the Academic Performance Rating Scale. *School Psychology Review, 20,* 284–300.

Fuchs, L. S., Fuchs, D., Hamlett, C. L., & Allinder, R. M. (1991). Effects of expert systems advice within curriculum-based measurement on teacher planning and student achievement in spelling. *School Psychology Review, 20,* 49–66.

Fuchs, L. S., Hamlett, C. L., & Fuchs, D. (1990a). *Monitoring basic skills progress: Basic reading* [Computer program]. Austin, TX: Pro-Ed.

Fuchs, L. S., Hamlett, C. L., & Fuchs, D. (1990b). *Monitoring basic skills progress: Basic spelling* [Computer program]. Austin, TX: Pro-Ed.

Gates, A. (1930). *Interest and ability in reading.* New York: Macmillan.

Gickling,. E. E., & Havertape, S. (1981). *Curriculum-based assessment (CBA).* Minneapolis, MN: School Psychology Inservice Training Network.

Hargis, C. H., Terhaar-Yonkers, M., Williams, P. C., & Reed, M. T. (1988). Repitition requirements for recognition. *Journal of Reading, 31,* 320–327.

Shapiro, E. (1996). *Academic skills problems: Direct assessment and intervention* (2nd ed.). New York: The Guilford Press.

Shinn, M. R. (1988). Development of curriculum-based local norms for use in special education decision-making. *School Psychology Review, 17,* 61–80.

Shinn, M. R. (1989). Curriculum-based measurement: Assessing special children. New York: The Guilford Press.

Turco, T. L., & Shear, S. M. (1991). Program for generating a direct-observation cue/response tape. *Journal of School Psychology, 29,* 405.

White, O. R., & Haring, N. G. (1980). *Exceptional teaching* (2nd ed.). Columbus, OH: Merrill.

Ysseldyke, J. E., & Christenson, S. L. (1987). *TIES: The Instructional Environment Scale.* Austin, TX: Pro-Ed.